BY THE MOON AND THE
ST

BY THE MOON AND THE STARS

A heart-rending, wartime story of a young
Czech exile's lonely struggle to grasp the
meaning of life and love

EVA HAYMAN

Random Century

Random Century New Zealand Ltd
(An imprint of the Random Century Group)

18 Poland Road
Glenfield
Auckland 10
NEW ZEALAND

Associated companies, branches and
representatives throughout the world.

First published 1992
© Eva Hayman 1992
ISBN 1 86941 158 7

Printed in Malaysia
by SRM Productions Services Sdn Bhd

CONTENTS

To my children, in memory of my parents

My gratitude goes to Kevin Convery for all his encouragement, to my daughter for correcting the manuscript and for choosing the title, and to Harriet Allan for her invaluable advice when editing the book.

We look before and after,
And pine for what is not:
Our sincerest laughter
With some pain is fraught;
Our sweetest songs are those that tell of saddest thought.

To a Skylark, by P.B. Shelley

PREFACE

Here is my story. I am a New Zealander by choice, and have had the privilege of living in this country since 1957. This book is taken from my diaries, written during the Second World War. I started to keep a diary in 1939 when, as a teenager, I was forced to leave Czechoslovakia. On seeing the shadow of disaster in the rise of Nazism enveloping our land, my parents sent my sister and me to England, the country that offered us shelter. My father's last words were: 'If the time ever comes when you cannot write to us, confide your thoughts and activities to a diary. And then, when all this is over, we shall be able to read it together and your mother and I shall not be completely deprived of that part of your life.'

Diligently, honestly, did I try to write for those who gave me life and for whose lives I feared for six long years.

When the devastating news of my parents' deaths in concentration camps reached me after the war ended in 1945, the diaries, written in Czech for them alone, were put away. For years and years the pain in my heart forbade me to touch the journals into which I had poured my soul. I did not open them again until forty years later. For my children, I summoned up the courage to translate them and face the most impressionable six years of my life – years that were so mixed with fear and hope, joy and despair. Yet it was more than that; from the vantage point of a secure life in New Zealand, I felt ready to re-read my story and to grasp the lessons learnt from a lonely youngster who survived. I was ready to yield to the compulsion to share my past with those sharing my present. This intention was strengthened in 1988 when I attended a reunion in England of those who escaped the Nazi terror in my country.

PART ONE

PART ONE

INTRODUCTION

In the heart of Europe, bordering Germany, Poland, Russia, Yugoslavia and Austria lies the land of my birth. Czechoslovakia is made up of Bohemia, Slovakia and Carpathia. Their history has been one of repression.

From the sixteeth century, for 400 years, the Habsburgs ruled over most of central and southern Europe, including what is currently called Czechoslovakia. The Czech nobility rebelled in 1618, only to be defeated two years later. In retaliation, the Habsburgs forcibly suppressed the Czech language and culture.

During the First World War the Czechs and Slovaks sided with the Allies and worked hard for the Czech cause. On 28 October 1918, the Czechoslovak Republic was proclaimed; the new Czechoslovakia was at last a democracy. Thomas Masaryk became its first, much-loved president and Eduard Beneš succeeded him in 1935.

In 1938 Hitler's armies marched into Austria, and later that year invaded the western part of Bohemia, Sudetenland. Hitler claimed that this move was justified because a large number of the people in Sudetenland had German origins and were German speakers. The British and French agreed that these borders of Czechoslovakia were to be ceded to Germany, and the English Prime Minister, Neville Chamberlain, announced that the agreement had secured 'Peace in our time'.

In March 1939, Hitler's armies moved into the capital city of Czechoslovakia, Prague, and Bohemia and Moravia became German Protectorates with Slovakia achieving an unsatisfactory independence. (What it meant to be a German 'Protectorate' was demonstrated later, when in 1942 the Protector, Reinhard Heydrich, was killed by Czech patriots, and in reprisal the Nazis demolished the central Bohemian village of Lidice and shot all its men.)

We were now told how to behave. This entailed obeying all the Germans' commands, ceding living space in our homes and schools to them, giving them anything they asked of us, and raising our hands in Hitler's salute. (Orders shouted in German still ring in my ears, making the German language – quite irrationally – abhorrent to me to this day.)

How the Nazis behaved towards the Jews had been typified already in 1938, the night that no Austrian or German Jew will forget, the night that is embedded in their memories and is called the 'Kristallnacht'. Nazis, in brown shirts and red armbands with swastikas on them, invaded and looted Jewish homes and businesses with no regard for life.

When the rumours of what was happening reached my country and my parents, it was hard to believe the atrocities described. My father could not accept that a civilized nation would allow such barbarous actions to go

1

unpunished; that the leader of the nation would not only allow but condone it was past his comprehension. Nevertheless, my parents' fears were aroused and convinced them that, should an opportunity present itself, they should try to send their two young daughters out of danger – to England.

So in June 1939, I was among 664 children who fled from Czechoslovakia after the German occupation of my country. Some of us went to English families, some to boarding schools, some to work. It was a brave gesture to take an unknown child for an unknown time. We knew nothing of the people involved in arranging our escape. The person chiefly responsible, Nicholas Winton, did not make himself known until forty-nine years later, when at a reunion of the survivors, I was finally able to meet him and say, 'Thank you for my life.' Without him and people like him I would not have survived, New Zealand would not be my home, my children would not have been born to taste the freedom of this land.

Nicholas now lives in retirement in Maidenhead and well remembers those days. He is the living proof of what one man can do for so many. At the end of 1938, he was thirty years old, living in a flat in London and working at the Stock Exchange. That year the jackbooted armies of Hilter were not only echoing but were feared all over Europe. Their tread spelt death and the end of freedom to the nations they occupied. The news of concentration camps and the inevitability of an early war resulted in a scramble of frantic refugees trying to leave their countries. A number of British organizations and agencies were attempting to help them. Before Christmas 1938, Nicholas Winton was to go skiing with his best friend, Martin Blake, but instead Martin asked Nicholas to follow him to Prague to help children in danger. Nicholas had studied in Germany and witnessed frequent beatings and persecution. He was aware of the urgency of the help needed and went to Prague immediately. He had found that it was possible to bring out children under the age of sixteen without their parents with a special British entry permit.

In Prague he scrounged a small office and before he could settle in there was a queue outside. The news had spread by word of mouth that there was an Englishman who could get the children out of danger. Nicholas recalls that the scene was heart-breaking: both rich and poor parents came to him for help. Nicholas drew up a list of the children and bombarded the Home Office for entry visas. When the visas were slow in coming he forged them. His days were hectic, his nights disturbed by distressed parents begging him to take their children. Although the Nazis were suspicious of his activities, the Czechs stubborn and the British somewhat slow in providing assistance, Mr Winton brought out 664 children before the war began. The children's terrified parents were willing to give them up rather than risk their lives under a Nazi tyrant.

Upon returning to London, Nicholas worked at the Stock Exchange in the daytime and spent the nights working for 'his' children. He sent all prospective foster parents photographs and a short curriculum vitae of six children for whom a home had to be found in England. He let them decide whose life would be saved. The urgency to get out as many children as possible increased

2

each day. Now, Nicholas says, looking back in anger, neither he nor anyone else could decide which case was the most urgent – all the children were in danger.

On 1 July 1939, a train left Czechoslovakia with the last group of children, 241 in total. Among them, hand in hand, sat my sister and I. Behind us, in our homeland, we had left our weeping parents, who had made this supreme sacrifice.

The story of my life is undoubtedly similar to the stories of hundreds of Jewish children who managed to escape from occupied countries, leaving their loved ones behind. It was for those loved ones that I faithfully wrote my diaries throughout the war. When letters to and from home ceased, the psychological need to pour my soul into the diaries became imperative, and I filled eleven notebooks. When I re-read these journals, I am aware of the firm bond binding me to my parents, especially to my father. It is a loving bond; yet it has never let me be free.

My mother (Irma) and father (Karel) together owned and managed a wine and liqueur import–export business. I well remember Mother's dream that she would be able to stay at home and clean and cook, especially cook; she was an artist at that. Being a business woman was not her idea of heaven. Father travelled from place to place buying and selling. He had friends everywhere and was known in our small town of Čelákovice by his first name. In those days only very close friends called each other by their first names, to do so was a mark of affection. Skilled at and devoted to the game of chess, Father spent each Saturday night in the Hospoda, a small Czech pub, playing until the early hours of the morning. Frequently at the weekends, my mother would visit her parents in Prague, often taking my sister Věra, who was four years my junior, and me with her.

I remember mother's father, my grandfather, Julius Kestner, as a bearded, old gentleman who recited poetry to me whilst standing with his back against a big brown stove. Matylda, my dear blind granny, cooked and baked in spite of her handicap and told me wonderful stories before I went to sleep. She spoke of St Wenceslav and of Jewish and Christian festivities, putting them in the context of stories about children.

I slept peacefully when in Prague, in my Aunt Berta's bed. She was Mother's unmarried sister. Intelligent and beautiful, she worked for an insurance firm and thought it her duty to look after her parents. Many a man's heart was broken because of this decision, and I often wonder how much her heart suffered, but she never complained. Mother's brother Gustav, the eldest in the family, was a lawyer in Prague. He and his wife Marta had two sons: Honza, my age, and Tomíček, Věra's age. Our cousins were bright, intelligent, polite and well behaved. Věra and I were country bumpkins compared to them. (They died in Aunt Berta's arms in Belsen Concentration Camp, as did my mother a few days later. Their parents and our grandparents also perished. Only Auntie Berta survived; to her sorrow she was condemned to life.)

3

We were closer to Mother's family than to Father's. My father's parents owned a little grocery shop in a small town called Suchdol. Father's favourite story was about his dog, which used to wait for him by the train each evening to welcome him back from the business college he attended in Prague. Before the First World War there were few Czech schools in Bohemia; my mother attended only German schools but Father went to a Czech high school. My father's father, Emil Diamant, died laughing at a game of cards when I was six years old. His wife, Emilie, died before I was born. I was named Eva Suzana Emilie. The first name was Auntie Berta's choice, the second my maternal grandfather's and the third my paternal grandfather's. My parents do not appear to have had a say!

Father had two sisters, Héda and Marta. Marta married Edwin Bloch and had a daughter, Héda, and son, Jirka. Father's other sister, Héda, married Joseph Kafka. I loved their two daughters, Máňa and Míša. (Míša was married and pregnant when she and her husband together with her parents and sister were sent to concentration camps. All except Héda Blochová, my cousin, perished.)

My memories are of a happy childhood in our small town. My sister Věra and I attended the local primary school, which, like our township, was predominantly Roman Catholic. A rabbi from Prague used to come every other Tuesday to give religious instruction to the children of the three Jewish families in Čelákovice. Sitting around our dining-room table would be my sister Věra, Marta, whose parents owned the grocery shop opposite our house, and two young boys, whose parents lived next door. I was the eldest in this unwilling group of learners. After the lessons, we walked to the station with the rabbi; when going to school I walked hand in hand with the local Catholic priest.

I loved school – my inquisitive mind assisted my eagerness to learn. At home we were surrounded by books. We discussed all our problems with our parents. Our comfortable home was not luxurious but was flooded with affection. Beggars never left the door without food and clothing; I remember one day Father, having gone to Prague to buy a few shirts, arrived home with only the old shirt on his back. On the way home he had met someone who needed the new ones more than he.

Tall and dark, my father was a handsome man. His shining hair and laughing eyes, his generous heart and friendly spirit endeared him not only to his family but to all the people in our small town. To his fourteen-year-old daughter he was an idol. I adored him, trusted him and with every fibre of my being wished to please him. My beautiful mother, with her dark brown eyes and curly brown hair, so gentle and fragile, was there ever a time when I did not feel a need to protect her? Father would punish us for our misdeeds, Mother never did. My love for her knew no bounds, she was the heart of our united family. My little sister, her fair hair falling on her shoulders, her blue eyes shining, was always full of life and mischief. We both experienced a happy childhood surrounded by relatives and friends, secure in the love of our parents.

4

I was also close to my special friend Pepik. We would walk and argue and now and then hold hands. Mstětická Silnice, a dusty road among the fields, was our favourite haunt. Pepik was a year older than me and a head taller. He had attractive brown eyes and wavy hair, and my heart went out to him because he had lost his father. Pepik and I had been friends for three years by the time I left Czechoslovakia. On 3 January 1939 I received his first gentle kiss by the river Elbe (Labe), our second favourite walk. On this day the meadows glistened under a carpet of white snow and the river moved silently under the cover of gleaming ice. 'If I cross the icy river without falling in, will you grant me a request?' Pepik asked. I nodded and watched my hero with bated breath, fervently praying he would not vanish in the cold waters. What his request would be I knew well. This, my first kiss, was as wonderful as I dreamt it would be. I felt so grown up. I confided my joy to my diary, where in those days I wrote only when important events took place. Though eager to tell my parents, I was not certain they would approve.

I vividly remember a moment in the preceding spring when I stopped in the town square on my way home from my music lesson. At midday the church bells were ringing and the singing birds were playing hide and seek among the leaves of huge oak trees standing majestically on each side of the cobbled road. The sun's rays warmed the meadow, full of daisies, daffodils and bluebells. I was intensely aware of overflowing with happiness – my heart was ready to burst, my soul was singing a thousand songs. Suddenly that moment passed and an unknown anguish entered my heart. 'So much joy cannot last,' I mused, 'but why this sudden fear of the future?'

In September 1938 Hitler annexed Sudetenland, the natural frontier of Czechoslovakia. The Czechs gave in to the pressure from England and France not to fight. Father's friends in France begged him to leave, stories of persecution of Jews in Germany and Austria crossed the frontier. 'I am a Jew, but I am a Czech first and foremost, I cannot just run away,' said Father. 'I fulfil God's law,' he once told me when I asked about his faith, 'by loving you, my children, and your mother, by doing good and trying not to harm anyone. To my faith I am bound by the grave of my parents.' So we stayed.

Thus in December 1938 we celebrated our last Christmas at home. We were Jewish, but a large Christmas tree stood in the middle of our sitting-room. Under the tree lay our presents to each other. As was the custom in our country we unwrapped our gifts on Christmas Eve after a meal of carp and all the traditional Czech trimmings – potato salad, peas, fresh salads – finishing with a beautiful cake full of fruit and almonds. The aroma of wood pervaded the room, for our pine tree was freshly cut the day before. I think on this last night we all felt a great love, a love enveloping the world of all people of every faith. As always, sharing our meal were a few friends from school who could not afford a Christmas treat. Little Věra wanted to bring her kittens inside, but their home was our loft. And in the yard on that night stood a brand-new, red bicycle, my present for Christmas and my fifteenth birthday, which followed on 1 January. How could one be sad on a night like this?

On 15 March 1939, when Hitler's armies entered Prague, my father was in the capital city. My memories are of sitting on our wide window-sill and waiting with Mother until the early hours of the morning for his homecoming. Father arrived a changed man, profoundly shaken by what he had experienced, and, for the first time, not sharing that experience with us. For the first time I knew real fear – of the unknown.

Soon there were German soldiers in our small town. People would disappear never to return, or to return with grey faces and grey hair. I was not sure what it all meant. My anxiety was entrusted to my diary not to my parents, as I did not want to worry them. Laughter had left their eyes. Then a large part of our school was confiscated for German soldiers. Our teachers instructed us to be careful of what we said while we worked in the overcrowded classrooms. Everybody had to learn German: the language in which orders were shouted in the streets and in the many homes confiscated by our enemy. I believe my father finally decided to try to send his daughters away when he found me arguing in my poor German with a Nazi soldier who was demanding something in the office of our business. I do not remember the details of the argument, only that I was hurriedly removed. I was fortunate that I encountered a German soldier who issued only a reprimand.

Then Auntie Berta told Mother of a British organization with a small office in Prague that was trying to send to England Czech children at risk who were under the age of sixteen. Mother filled in the forms, took our photographs and applied for us to leave. She did not believe that we would be chosen, for hundreds of parents were seeking escape for their children and only a few could go.

A few months before Hitler's armies marched into Czechoslovakia, our family was baptized into the 'Hus' church, a Czech Protestant church, in a vague hope that this might ease our plight as Jews. I went to bed at night saying my Jewish prayer and the Lord's Prayer, for I believed the Almighty understood the complexities of religion. I had a great faith in the God of all peoples. We never found out whether having been baptized was part of the reason that Věra and I were so quickly selected. Later, I learnt only that my guardian chose me for my smile and because I was a good student. All we were told was to be ready to leave on 29 June 1939.

'Only for a short time,' we kept saying to ourselves. 'Our country will soon be free and we shall be able to return. At least we shall learn English.' As far as I remember, we had only three to four weeks to get ready, if not less. Mother was furiously busy, providing us with new wardrobes, some of which she sewed herself. She thought of everything; I wore those clothes for years. Now, fifty years later, I still own a treasured and much-faded blue towelling cape. Mother was proud of it, my friends admired it, it kept me warm and dry and eventually my children used to hide underneath it on our way back from the beach.

I went to school up to my last day in Czechoslovakia. I was heart-broken having to say goodbye to my classmates and teachers. 'Don't drown in the English sea; remember always that you are a Czech. It would be a shame if our

6

nation lost a person like you,' said Professor Hlináček. I had always been fond of him and felt very proud at this. I was not going to disappoint him. By now I was at the 'gymnasium', a Czech high school. One of our gymnastic organizations, Sokol, also gave me a special farewell. My friends came to our house and so did our relatives. It could have been exciting – Věra and I were the centre of attention – but my heart was heavy with premonition.

Parting from Pepik was hard. He promised to keep an eye on my parents, as did a few other faithful friends. They adhered to their promises, even when mixing with Jews was forbidden and visiting them unheard of. Somehow Mother was the strong one during this time. She was busy with preparations, while Father was the silent onlooker. I wanted to kiss his sad eyes as I was telling him not to worry and not to worry about us. I promised to be a mother to Věra, I would not let them down.

On our last day, I said goodbye to Věra's cats in the loft and gave a last slice of bread and salt and a few lumps of sugar to Vanica Bella, our horse, which had carried me on many an adventure. We were permitted to take only clothes with us. However, Mother, trusting luck, put a tiny platinum ring on my finger and a little golden cross around my neck as a concession to our baptism. This was accompanied by a Jewish medallion and a tiny ivory elephant for luck. I wonder what a Gestapo soldier would have thought had he peered under my jumper.

When everything was neatly packed in our cases, Father asked if I would permit him and Mother to read the diary into which I had written spasmodically over the last year. In it I had voiced all my anger against the German invasion. Such writings were not safe to be carried in case our luggage was searched, but I had packed the diary with my few other possessions. For the last time Father was angry with me – which relieved the tension – and everything had to come out of my case in order to retrieve the diary buried at the bottom. Into the diary's pages I had poured out my young soul, my joys and sorrows. I had spoken of my affection for Pepik and of my intense love for my parents and how hard it was to tell them of those feelings. I was always grateful that I had written this, and grateful that they had read it after our departure. They buried this diary in the garden, where I found it after the war.

We paid a last visit to our grandparents in Prague. Our family did not own a car, but I remember arriving in one at my grandparents' flat. Father, who did not drive, must have hired a taxi. In the taxi we ate dairy-milk chocolate with nuts. After the Nazi invasion Mother decided to store as much food as possible in case of food shortages, and this chocolate was part of her collection. Now, should the need arise, her daughters would not be there to eat the chocolate saved for them.

Our grandparents had prepared a festive meal for us, but no one seemed to eat. By now I felt excitement and fear, a mixture of emotions difficult to cope with. Our two cousins, Honza and Tomíček and their parents came to say *bon voyage*. Both the boys fervently hoped to be on the next transport to England. (As fate would have it, ours was the last.)

7

Everyone was talking as if they believed that the precaution of sending us away would prove to be futile, that the Germans would retreat and we would return home in the not too distant future. But the pain in their eyes belied my parents' words. 'We shall manage no matter what,' Father had said a few days earlier to me. 'Without you, one burden will be lifted for me, for I shall know that you and Věra are safe. I could not bear it if you were to suffer here when I had this opportunity to send you away.'

There used to be so much joy and love in our family; now, at the moment of parting, the joy turned to sorrow. But the strength of love pervaded everything. The tears running from my granny's blind eyes felt hot on my cheeks as she kissed and hugged me; our grandfather's beard tickled as always when he gave me his last kiss, but this time I did not tease him nor did I laugh. The two dear faces stood at the window waving, Granny with her unseeing eyes. Auntie Berta came with us to the station. It was dark by then, for the train was leaving at midnight. I remember shivering, though the June night was warm.

The railway station was full of parents with anxious faces and swarms of children, some of whom were crying bitterly. The small talk was to allay our pain. 'You will write and write often,' Father said. Then the last hug, the last kiss and we boarded the train. Mother, Father and Auntie Berta stood at the station as the train moved off, carrying over 200 Czech children.

As we were leaving, Mother had whispered, 'Look at the stars at night – the moon and the stars will be the messengers of our love. You are a real treasure, a real diamond (our surname in Czech was Diamant, and Diamantová is the feminine version). Oh Mother! My darling mother, how I wished to take your pain upon myself. And Father, how much older he looked and how grey he had become. I remembered his last words:

If the time ever comes when you cannot write to us, confide your thoughts
and activities to a diary. And then, when all this is over, we shall be able
to read it together, and your mother and I shall not be completely deprived
of that part of your life. There is so much that I have tried to teach you,
there is so much more I wished to tell you. Much love I have given you
and so much more is stored in my heart for you.

Oh, Father! We thought we had a lifetime of sharing ahead of us. I was not ready to grow up, not so suddenly. In my hand was the hand of my little sister. She was to be my first consideration from then on. Yet neither of us knew where we were going, how far from each other, which part of England or with whom we were to share our lives. Our tears did not come until our parents disappeared from view. I waved and waved; a farewell to them and to my childhood for ever – although I did not know it then.

PART TWO

What follows are excerpts from my diaries translated into English from Czech, the language in which they were written. They begin in June 1939 on my last day in Czechoslovakia and take me through to the devastating day in July 1945 when I learnt of my parents' deaths. My diaries are too long to translate in full, so I have edited them and in places have interspersed the entries with summaries of events.

PART TWO

TO BE BRAVE REQUIRES
A GREAT DEAL OF
HARD WORK

28.6.1939 Čelákovice
I will write this new diary in England; I am compelled to leave my old diary
at home. We leave tomorrow night and will arrive in England on 1 July.
How I wish that the rest of this diary could be written here, how I hope
that I will be allowed to return soon, very soon, to my homeland.

9.7.1939 Dorset
I am in England, a land so many people dream of. For me this is not the
best land, the country of my dreams can only be my Czech land. I have no
idea when I shall return. When, at the end of the last school year at home,
we remembered Jan Hus, our national hero, I felt so dreadfully sad, I could
not help crying. I promised myself never to shed tears at school again. But
then I never dreamt that the time would come when I would have to leave
all those I love so much without knowing when – or if – I will be able to
return to them. Not even in my worst nightmares did I dream that this
would happen.
  I was broken-hearted on the last day at Sokol when I had to dance with
each member and all of them wished me a happy journey and an early
return. The chief 'sister' gave me a national flag so that I would not forget.
How could I ever forget? The flag is hanging above my bed, and I look
at it before I go to sleep every night. Then I gaze at the skies, kiss the
photographs of my parents, my sister and my friend Pepik. The last with a
little bit of guilt; would Father be angry? You would not, would you, my
father? There cannot be much wrong in being fond of a nice boy who,
besides you, is the best friend I have. You have no idea how much it hurt
me on our last day at home when, because I had arrived a little late, you
said, 'It seems to me that any Pepik is dearer to you than your father.'
There is no one whom I could love more than I love you and my mother.
And even had I loved Pepik a great deal it is not the kind of love I feel for
you. Do you understand me, my old friend? I cried bitterly that you should
think that of me, but I found refuge in your arms. It hurt me more than it
would have hurt you to have known that I told an untruth in answer to
your question whether I cried when parting from Pepik. I did not wish to
tell a lie, but felt I could not tell you of the bitter tears I had shed. I

wanted to get rid of every tear in my body so that there would be no tears left in the evening when I had to part from you. I wanted you and Mother to have only my smile to remember me by; my breaking heart you were not to see.

And that is how I left you on 29 June 1939 from Masaryk Station in Prague. The machine without feelings did not know that it was carrying children away from their parents, the parents who would be crying at the loss of their greatest joy and who did not know whether to believe that a better future beckoned their children. I looked into the darkness and thought of all the friends and relations who parted from us with tears in their eyes. Will I ever return? Will I ever see them again? I felt my parents' pain as well as my own as I hugged little Věra, who, exhausted, finally fell asleep.

When we arrived in the Czech township of Terezín, our leaders remembered that they had left something in Prague and hurried to retrieve it in a taxi, keeping us waiting for three and a half hours. The little ones cried. Then we left Czechoslovakia.

I felt so very sad, I kept thinking of how my dearest parents had stood in front of the train making such a great effort not to shed tears in front of us. Their children were leaving them, to whom will they go? How will they fare? Will they be happy? Those questions must have occupied their thoughts. They must have asked themselves: When will they return? Will they ever return? Shall we meet again? And I too was asking: Shall we meet again? When and how, under what conditions? So many had said, 'Do not forget us, do not forget that you are a Czech.' How could I possibly forget? Pepik, too, had said, 'Happy journey, I'll be with you in my thoughts.' Would it be possible to forget all these dear people? The train was charging ahead and I was remembering, thinking of everyone and everything I had left behind.

When we reached Germany, I was shaken by fear. The darkness outside contributed to my feeling of impotence and anger. This country, whose soldiers invaded my land, was the cause of our separation. I held my breath wondering if our luggage was being searched. They did not search our persons, but I was not the only one to relax upon reaching the safe haven of Holland.

In Holland they gave us cocoa and bread and cheese. We looked at the little houses and fields from the train windows until we arrived at the Port of Rotterdam. At 11pm, eleven hours after we left Prague, we walked on to the ship that was to take us to England across the British Channel. Exhausted, Věra and I fell asleep at once. At about 5.30am I woke up and soon Věra's gaze joined mine on the calm waters of the sea, sparkling under the first rays of the rising sun. So this was the sea! I witnessed its glory for the first time. My country is surrounded by land. The vastness and the beauty of the ocean took my breath away, and silently I wished that our parents could share this moment with their two daughters. Then we arrived in Harwich. Věra and I. Two children among so many others. Two great patriots, whose national flag hangs above their beds, now found themselves in England.

It took the whole afternoon before we were free from being counted and all the other checks, then we boarded the train that carried us to London. Here we were taken to a great big hall, and they called out our names. Mine was called before Věra's, and I was bitterly disappointed not to have seen who was to take care of her. Two old ladies were waiting for me. They allowed me to say goodbye to my little sister, then we went by train to Sandecotes School in Parkstone, Dorset, where I am a boarder. There are boarders and day-girls here, but I shall write about the school another time. I keep seeing my darling little sister looking so forlorn; I do so wish we could be together. I feel myself to be such a pawn in the wind of fate. Věra and I lead our own lives at home, but we do love each other and these last few weeks have brought us very close. I do so want to help her, look after her – will this be possible across the miles?

Later I discovered that the two ladies who collected me were teachers at my new school. They had come because they could speak German and were sent by Miss Dunn, the headmistress of the school and my guardian. She knew that I could communicate in German; my English being non-existent.

Hoping that our exile might be for a short time only, surrounded by kind people and finding that one can communicate a great deal by using gestures and expressions as well as a dictionary, I did not feel as isolated as I thought I would be. From the moment we learnt that we were to leave our parents, there was much to do and little time to think. The journey to England tired me, and the new impressions left me bewildered. Until now I had obeyed my parents' wishes and shared my experiences with them through letters. It was when the excitement wore off and the enormity of the path the world was choosing had sunk in that my constant fear for those at home and my unshakable loneliness began. Thus the first few days were just an adventure.

As Věra did not know where I would be living and I did not have her address before leaving home, our first task consisted of sending our addresses to our parents who then sent mine to Věra and *vice versa*. At that time we did not wonder why we had to be parted, we were considered to be two fortunate sisters who escaped Nazism. The truth was that Nicholas Winton had his time cut out placing us all with guardians, any other consideration was impossible.

Sandecotes was a luxurious school for girls. My parents would not have been able to afford to send me there. The school was owned by a church trust that offered me a free place, and Miss Dunn, the headmistress, was responsible for my every-day needs. Tall and slim with greyish hair and dark-rimmed glasses, my guardian appeared 'very English' to me. This was confirmed in my eyes by the fact that she carried her Scottie dog wherever she went! At home I had rarely seen a Scottish terrier, and it was unthinkable that a headmaster there would be seen with one.

The school itself consisted of a number of buildings that housed dormitories and a large school house in the midst of the most beautiful garden. The garden was tended by Mr Jones, who very quickly became my friend. Not only did he give me flowers, which spoke volumes, but he also encouraged me to believe that my sojourn in England would not last too long.

A week after our arrival in England, I received the first letters from home. There was only a short note from Mother, who was beside herself with joy to know that Věra and I were with good people, even though we were far apart. My sister was with a delightful family in Bootle, Liverpool, and sounded happy. Mother wrote also that she cried with happiness and so did our friends and relatives when they heard her news. Father wrote a longer letter:

My Soul,
Believe me that as a soldier I have experienced much in the last war, but nothing can be compared to my feelings after your departure until your first letter arrived. You can hardly imagine my joy when Mother telephoned me to say that both you and Věra had written to us. I was away on business, but at once left everything and hurried home to read your wonderful letters over and over again. By now everyone in Čelákovice has read your letters, and just as they cried with us when you left so they all laughed with us when reading your pages. Věra is a fine girl . . . she writes well and sounds sensible. I really do not need to worry about either of you and I do believe you when you write that both of you are surrounded by kind people. So I believe that in this way the Almighty is repaying to you all the good that Mother and I might have bestowed upon others in the past. I was delighted with your letter, especially when you stated that you are well and happy and that you will study and study gladly. Can you remember my saying to you that the greatest gift a father can give to his child is knowledge and wisdom? Money and possessions a person can lose, but what you hold in your head and heart no one can take away from you. And so you can never feel lost.

I am so glad that I have such a fantastic girl for my daughter. I know that you will always be a real diamond and that in spite of your young years you will face everything with courage. We long for your letters, please write at least once a week. Auntie Berta is coming from Prague to copy your letters for your grandparents and for the rest of the relatives . . .

You must know by now that everything you write is of great interest to us, nothing can be boring. And, my darling, you must bear in mind that each word you write is a greeting to me. After all, you do know how much love holds for you.
Your Táta (Father)

I was kept busy writing home, to my sister, to my friends, and in my diary:

14

It was not until I had Mother's letter that I learnt no one came for Věra until the next day. My eleven-year-old sister was taken by a kind, rich lady to her home where she awaited the arrival of her guardian, a Mrs Rainford from Liverpool. Věra writes that she is having a good time, is happy and not at all homesick because she dreams of home every night. I do hope that I shall see her during the school holidays. I think they start in one month's time, but am not sure.

From home I am receiving wonderful letters, full of encouragement. But I think that our parents need the encouragement and comfort even more than I do. From Pepik I have received one letter so far. I was afraid that he might not have received my note – in it I expressed my feelings for him and confided that I am at times very lonely. I would not like my mother and father to know that.

Every night I watch the stars and think of home. I write letters to all those I love. They are full of hope and faith that our tomorrows will be happier, and yet I fear that it may not be so. I must not be afraid, I must be brave. Today my father has written how proud he was of his brave daughter. And this daughter must not disappoint him, she must be courageous. And my mother, her letter was so full of love. Yet I could feel her hidden sadness, which Pepik saw in her eyes when he went to read my letter to her. Pepik wrote that he felt such peace in the presence of my parents, he found it hard to express his feelings. I wish I could have been there. Pepik also writes that he visits places where we walked and thinks of me and feels that in our thoughts we are together.

Yes, yes! Every free moment I think of home. I am with all of you there, at home. My grandparents, aunties, friends, they all wish me happiness. I like it here, people are kind, but I can be really happy only with my parents at home.

I have friends here, but so far no close friends. I am closest to Pia, a girl from Yugoslavia. She is about two years my senior. I think she was asked to keep an eye on me! I felt I could trust her until I read (and should not have) in her letter written in German to her parents that I am very pleasant and don't look Jewish but ask too many questions. I wish she had told me that my incessant questioning worries her. Everything is so new and so strange and she is the only one among the girls with whom I can communicate in German. No one speaks Czech. Somehow it hurt.

The English girls seem cold. I cannot understand them and feel a stranger among them. Anyhow, I believe that they mean well and that I will get used to their ways. I shall learn new ways, but will not forget the old ones.

My belief that I shall live the rest of my youth at home again, that after bad times good will return, gives me strength.

21.7.1939
It is summer but the weather is awful outside. In the room where we do our homework there is no one but me. So I turn to you, my diary. The fire in

15

the fireplace warms my feet, in spite of which I shiver at times with an uneasy pang of sadness. I keep thinking of my parents and all those I love, and I fear that I shall never see them again. I try to get rid of those thoughts and am angry with myself for thinking so.

I write to Pepik about my feelings and that at times I no longer believe in a happy outcome. To my parents I write happy letters, full of faith in our reunion, I write the same to my little sister. As for myself? I so need courage and someone who would take me in their arms, press my hand and say, 'Courage, courage, all will be well again.'

I had a letter from the chief sister in Sokol. She wrote, 'Be brave and do not forget.' To be brave requires a great deal of hard work. But to forget? How could I ever forget? I keep remembering, I think of them all the time.

The day before yesterday I went home with a girl who is a day-girl here, called Suzanne. Her parents will take care of me for fourteen days during the coming holiday. They have a huge garden, a huge house and are very kind. After afternoon tea we went for a walk and I was taken in a luxurious car back to school. They were so genteel, my people whom I love are rough by comparison. But they all seem to be honest.

Věra wrote that she was going to visit me this month. I was so happy and at once wrote about it to our parents. At the same time I had this feeling that it would not come off. Too true, my sister made a mistake, she is coming next month.

I am beginning to understand English a bit more, so I do not sit in the classroom as a dummy. Even some of the English food seems more palatable, but I still cannot stand the rhubarb pie on Sundays. Wiltshire, the waiter, very kindly removes my full plate when the mistress sitting at the head of the table is not looking.

O n Sundays we all went to church wearing our Sunday uniform, including a hat. (School uniform was unknown in my country.) As a beret was the only headgear I had ever allowed to rest on my unruly hair, even in the winter when skiing and skating in the cold, a hat felt very uncomfortable. We had to parade in front of the matron to demonstrate how well dressed we were. My hat bounced somewhat above my forehead. I well remember the matron pulling it nearer to my eyes – and me pushing the hat up again. Not understanding the language well seemed a great asset in this tug of war. Eventually I gave in, only until I turned the corner! Although my grasp of English had improved, in church I could not understand a word. And so sitting there I dreamt my dreams.

That I did make reasonable progress in learning this language, which is spoken so differently from the way it is written, was due to Miss Vinall. Over thirty years old, already a little bent, for Miss Vinall was an arthritis sufferer, with reddish hair and blue eyes, this kind teacher became my friend for life. She not only taught me English in the classroom but gave so much of her free time to wander with the young stranger in the garden, point to flowers, grass and trees, and explain. We would sit on the lawn with pen and paper and my little Czech–English dictionary. She answered my endless questions patiently. 'English is the only language without any rules,' I used to complain. 'Yes,' she would agree, 'we say things in a certain way, but I was never asked before *why* we say it so.' Many expressions puzzled me. For example, 'Will you come with me for a walk?' was by my standards a question not as demanding as: 'Eva, come with me for a walk'. And I could not make sense of a 'stable' government and a 'stable' for horses. I used to imagine all the parliamentarians eating hay in a stable. Miss Vinall would smile as I tried to explain my dilemmas.

When, after the first year at school, our paths diverged, my letters to her were returned corrected with red ink! Never did she cease to be my favourite tutor. Our correspondence continued until her death a few years ago. Even at the age of eighty, Miss Vinall was teaching English to foreigners, assuring me that her technique had much improved since 1939.

My diary testifies to my great relief that my sister settled happily with her English family, Mr and Mrs Rainford and their daughter Dorothy. I still hold on to one or two of Věra's letters, wishing I had kept them all. In July 1939 the eleven year old had written:

Dear Eva

How are you? Tomorrow I'll write home. I am not at all homesick, do you know why? Each night I dream that I am at home with our mother. Once I dreamt that I stood outside our house with my friend Marta and the boy Zdeněk. And Zdeněk said, 'Someone – the person next door – promised us a pig. They are going to wash in the river not only the pig but also Věra and Eva's horse, Vanica. I think they want to drown them. When they walk past us, can you catch the pig by its tail, Marta?' And Marta replied, 'I would rather catch the horse, she has more meat on her.' And then I woke up. That was funny, don't you think? What a dream!

For my birthday I received boxes of chocolates and a necklace and all sorts of other things. Girls and boys who are strangers to me gave me presents. In the evening I was given a cake with candles on it. They lit the candles and later I blew them out. I write home twice a week and am having a really good time.

A birthday cake with candles was an unknown tradition to us. I was pleased that my sister was surrounded with kindness. I knew that her happiness would alleviate some of my parents' fears.

23.7.1939
It is Sunday. I have written home. Just now the feeling of despondency will not leave me. Letters – the silent words – do not seem enough. I long to

hear my parents' voices, feel their arms around me. I am surrounded by kind and rich people, life would be much harder if they were unkind, but their smiles say to me, 'Poor little girl, you must be brave.' I so wish to hear, 'No need to be sad, all will be well very soon.'

Each night I kiss the photos of my parents and Věra and wish them joy, courage and happiness; I tell them not to be sad, not to worry. Then I put the photos away and send my greetings to my loved ones by the stars. I say my prayers and beg God Almighty to grant our wish of early reunion.

I have never prayed so hard before, can You hear me, God? I realize now what comfort it is to have faith in You. Please, do not be angry when at times I do not know what to do, when life seems bleak and I am helpless. You know me better than I know myself, You know of the pain in my heart, You know of my dreams. Will You fulfill them? Please God, don't deprive me of my faith, grant me courage and strength. I feel so mixed up, if only I could speak with someone from home.

25.7.1939

Today I wrote to Věra, and then Pia brought me two letters from home and one from Pepik. My mother wrote with reference to a book I received from her, and for which I had thanked her. She said, 'I had sent it without telling Father, but he was so happy when you wrote saying how thrilled you were with it.' How could it be otherwise? I browsed through the book about Slet (a small version of the Olympics for Slav nations where gymnasts from Sokol took part) and lived over and over again the happy days of a year ago when I was one of the participants. I was delighted with my parents' letters, I always am. I could visualize them writing to us, trying to convey joy to us. And Pepik wrote that he wants to make life easier, or rather more worthwhile, by working for our country. He believes our aims and dreams to be the same.

F rom my brave little sister I was also receiving delightful letters:

I am going to school soon, I wonder what it will be like. The lady with whom I live gives me money sometimes. Eva, I am saving! I have five pounds, one shilling and five pence. We understand each other by using our hands and using the dictionary. I am starting to enjoy the food. I have not had a bath yet. They give me stamps. I shall wear the same clothes to school as everyone else. The photo of Mother and Father I keep in an album. Thank you for the photo that you sent me.

I write home twice a week. I do not call the lady here 'Mother'. Give my greetings to your new friends, but do not forget the old ones. Eva, write again soon. Lots of kisses.

From your Věra

26.7.1939

I had to finish yesterday, the 'gong' went and we had some kind of a celebration. I forgot to say that Pepik also wrote that the Germans are demanding our wheat and other agricultural products; that they appear to rob us of the last possessions we have. Almost the last, because our hope, faith and thoughts can never be taken away from us, but I do hope that the Germans will leave my people their hard-earned bread. I do not intend to change my own thoughts, but I am realizing that it is not that easy to remain a hard-headed Czech. It must be easy for me, I must find joy in belonging to my little nation. I must not forget what I had promised to myself when I was leaving – that I shall remain a Czech, that Czechoslovakia will be my only homeland. I told Professor Hlinovský at my school: 'I'll not turn into an English lady.' I must keep my word. By being genuine, straightforward (as the Czechs), I should get as far as the English do by being genteel.

I don't know what is happening to me just now. Suddenly I feel a little happier. I am so looking forward to my holiday. I shall be spending fourteen days in the home of seventeen-year-old Suzanne and fourteen days with Monica, who is sometimes called Bunty. She is sixteen years old and very nice to me. I spoke (sort of) with her parents last night, but have not yet met her nineteen-year-old brother.

1.8.1939

So I find myself with Suzanne. It is beautiful here. I have my own room and a loan of a bicycle. Suzanne is so nice. Her mother and an old aunt are at home, her father is at present in France. They also have a gardener, housemaid, chauffeur with his wife and eight-year-old son, a dog and birds.

I feel almost happy here, for I felt so sad at the celebration at the end of the school year when everyone elses' parents were present. It was a so-called 'Speech Day'. The bishop came and gave out the prizes. I could understand a little when he spoke. The girls performed some kind of dancing, and after that the parents inspected our work (drawings, essays, etc) done during the year. I say 'our', yet I had been here only four weeks. I met other girls' parents. One man spoke to me in Russian (which I did not understand), and told me that he had visited Prague. When I was going to sleep that day I felt quite content. However, the sadness returned on Thursday when I had to pack my things. I kept remembering packing my possessions at home and unpacking them here and the feeling of loneliness and desolation. Somehow the other girls' laughter and conversation about their homes were painful to me. But Miss Dunn called me to her and gave me stamps and money. She spoke so very nicely to me and I loved her very much at that moment. I can see that she is very kind and I am grateful to her for the way she, so simply, gives me things. She does not make me feel it is a present for which I *have* to be grateful, for I know that I am not likely ever to be able to repay her for her kindness.

Suzanne was a gentle girl, not at all spoilt by what I saw as great wealth, a large garden, big house, tennis court and a chauffeur-driven car. To find myself surrounded by such riches seemed like a dream. More than the riches, the kindness bestowed on me by everyone remains a part of my memory to this day.

I understood that Miss Dunn asked the pupils if anyone would give me a home for a short time during the school holidays. And so it was decided that I would spend fourteen or so days with Suzanne and fourteen days with Monica (Bunty) Allner. After that I would travel from Poole in Dorset to Liverpool in Lancashire to spend the rest of the summer holiday with my sister and her English family.

Suzanne's and Bunty's families knew each other well, so I was introduced to the Allners before spending the second fourteen days with them. Mrs Allner, with her straight black hair, was tall and well-proportioned and about ten years younger than her husband, whom I considered elderly (he was about fifty years old). Grey-haired, with a kindly smile and almost always a pipe either in his hand or between his lips, Mr Allner was so unlike my father in looks, but so like him in the great affection he bestowed on me for the rest of his life.

I thought Bunty very pretty and always in a hurry, though she was patience itself when trying to explain something to me. Cedric, her brother, came for this holiday from Oxford, and in my diary I remarked: 'A ready-made brother. I have always wished I had an older brother. And Cedric has a sailing boat. Not even in my dreams did I imagine that one day I would sail on the ocean.' Whilst with Suzanne I saw a great deal of Bunty and Cedric, as well as Desmond. Desmond was the only son of Mrs Lansdown, a widow. During these holidays he was Suzanne's faithful companion. Fair-haired and tall, Desmond was to join the air force never to return.

2.8.1939

Here at Suzanne's everyone is very kind. This afternoon we went for a picnic. Accompanying us were three of her aunties and the chauffeur. The countryside is extremely beautiful. I looked towards the east and thought of home. The English countryside is so much greener than ours. I suppose something good must come from all the rain they get here.

Today I received five letters. Two from my parents, one from Věra, one from Pepik and one from Libuše – a schoolfriend. The post is very bad – letters seem to take longer to reach me than they used to. My mother writes beautifully. As always her letter is full of love for us. Mother has copied for me Miss Dunn's letter to her and added that this letter put her mind at rest and made her very happy. Miss Dunn wrote:

Dear Mr and Mrs Diamant,
Thank you for your letter. I can assure you that Eva is already quite accustomed to our way of life. Her grasp of the English language is very good and I am sure that she will speak it fluently before long. Do not worry

about her, we shall keep her for a few years and will make sure that she leaves prepared for life's journey. Eva is a very intelligent girl and will not get lost in the world. I am in contact with Věra's guardian, Mrs Rainford, and we hope to make arrangements which will enable the sisters to spend part of their holidays together. I do sympathize with you that you had to part from your children and I hope that there are many happy days in store for you.

Yours sincerely M. Dunn

I remember being allowed to read the letter written to Miss Dunn by my parents. They, who were so proud and always the givers, were gracious and humble when accepting charity for their children. Their hope was that one day they would be able to recompense a little for the kindness bestowed on us.

I continued my diary with reference to the letter from my friend, Libuše:

Libuše believes that I shall return soon and is glad that I have not forgotten them. Like me, Libuše remembers the happy days at school. So many of us had to leave. When shall we meet again, if at all?

My father has written me a lovely, beautiful letter. Besides other things, he wrote that he is worried about my intense patriotism and my friendship with Pepik. Father says, 'You can remain a Czech patriot, but you must be prepared to cease feeling so if the time should come when the Czech people would not include you in their ranks, would not think of you as a Czech. Then, I want to be the only one without a home, you and Věra must think of England as your home, the country which opened her arms to you and whose people have treated you so kindly.' About Pepik Father writes, 'It is not selfishness that bids me to ask you to love me only. I so wish to save you from much pain, because if it were not possible for you to return, your hopes, your dreams would be all in vain. There would be no happiness for you here. I believe that in you I have a real jewel.'

Further my father wrote that he loves Věra and me equally, but that I always needed much love and he gave me so much of it and has so much more love in store for me. Father's beautiful letter made me happy, but also a little sad. I do hope my answer does not cause him pain. Here is a copy of my letter:

Dearest Father,

Thank you for your wonderful letter. I have read it many times and I shall go on reading it over and over again. I hope that I can understand all that you have written. I am so glad that you do not regret sending us to England. I know that at home we would be of no help to you or anyone else. Here we are with kind people who understand what it means to be away from home, what it means not to know when we shall return – if we'll ever return to you. Perhaps they are even more worried on our behalf than I am. I am trying to put sadness aside, it does not help and only makes life harder. And I do not wish to be promising only in words that I shall be a good student. I want to prove to you that I will learn and study as best I can. I want to prove it to you and to Mother and to Miss Dunn who is so kind to me.

And I wish to show what a Czech girl can do so that my nation can be proud of me. Father dearest, my love for my country is embedded deep in my heart. Until your letter, it never occurred to me that the Czechs would ever deny me, that I could not call myself a Czech and a member of Sokol. That would hurt dreadfully, but even then I would not cease to love my country. I do believe that the one who loves his country, who believes that his native land is his home, can never be a refugee without a homeland. Yet, whatever happens in the future, I shall always obey you and Mother, no matter how far away you may be. After all, I know that my grey-haired friend and worried mother have only our good in their hearts. And if I ever can do anything for you, I shall always be ready to do so. I believe all children wish to recompense their parents. And, no matter what I do for you, I could never repay you for all that you have done and are doing for us.

You have sent us to a foreign land knowing how much you will miss us. You have sent us away because you thought only of our happiness. Fate works in a mysterious way, no one knows what will be, and maybe that is a good thing. I do believe that we shall meet again, that Věra and I will return, and above all I trust my own will and strength. To have to stand on my own two feet does not hurt anymore, I am proud of it, proud on your behalf.

You do not need to be sad that now you are not able to contribute directly to our upbringing. We had a good start, you have given us a strong foundation on which to build, and your letters guide us in the way you wish us to continue life's journeying.

Father dear, do not fear that with my patriotism I shall insult the English people. Everyone is proud of their nation, and they have a right to be proud of England. The people I have met so far are extraordinarily kind. I do so hope that I shall always meet kind people only. Our President Masaryk has said: 'To love your country does not mean that you do not honour the countries of others.' And I so esteem the English people, not only because they have accepted me with such kindness but also because I see their goodwill to help where help is needed. Politics I do not understand, so I cannot sit in judgement on anyone.

I do so want to be able to march only forward, hold my head high, not be afraid and not give in. Maybe life will show me that it is not as easy as I imagine; maybe one day I shall shed bitter tears and think of the days when I could cope with pain and difficulties, when my will to be brave did not let me down. I do believe that in this life which so many call hard, everyone finds some happiness and joy. And where does a child not find joy, where does not laughter grow for the young? But, no matter where I am, no matter what I do, I shall always follow your bidding.

You write that you are also worried by my friendship with Pepik. Please believe me, Pepik is my best friend. Do not be afraid, between us are no promises of faithfulness. I am very fond of him, perhaps more than pure friendship allows. He always listened patiently to my worries, explained many things, and I learned a great deal from him. I want this friendship to last for ever. I know, Father dearest, that I am a child and that there is plenty of time left for me to be what one calls 'in love'. And I do want to obey you and have room for learning in my head. But, if I am not compelled to, I shall not forget. I am a child, my father, perhaps a somewhat older child, but one full of hope. I remember when I wrote in some homework that a child sees the world through rose-coloured spectacles. I do try not to take off the pink glasses too often and wish that they would cover my sight permanently.

Perhaps this year I have lived through more events than many have done in twenty years, but I think this has not affected me so as to change me. I must persist, I must win, I must believe in my own strength. And again your Eva has a smile playing around her lips. God is kind, and my faith in Him is so strong. After all, if there was no pain in the world, would we value joy? And I thank God that I can bear the pain, that my faith in a happy future always wins with me.

I do hope that you can understand my letter, you and my dearest mother, that you cease to worry about my patriotism and my friendship and that you do believe that I am only yours,
Eva

My father's answer written on 1 August 1939 was as follows:

My soul,
I have given you all the love a father can give to his child; with an unselfish love did I bring you up, but by a far more beautiful love am I being rewarded: a love that stems from a young girl's pure soul. Your letter, my dearest, is as a gift from heaven, your words songs of angels, more than a hymn, more than a prayer. A treasure is your every word, a diamond each sentence, your philosophy is as a wonderful kingdom to me. You are all mine, your soul, your heart, even your magnanimity.

This last year has seen my child grow into a young girl, the last day of your sojourn at home turned this daughter into a young woman. I keep seeing you on the last afternoon at home, then at your grandparents' home, and at the end of the day in the train. I keep seeing your dear head pressed against the window of the train. I am unable to forget the look in your eyes at the moment when the train started moving, your eyes that were begging, saying, 'Mother, Father do not give in, be brave, hold on.'

We did not collapse nor did our Eva collapse. We shall stand fast till the happy end.

You understand so well, you are so accomplished in everything. In your patriotism, in your friendships, in your grasp of life. You are sensible, strong in your faith and courage, and wise and kind. No more do I fear for you and no more do I fear for Věra. As we may not be able to, I know you will be a good teacher to her and be her guardian.

Your love is for your mother and me. What joy for us! Believe me that in this world there is nothing more beautiful than the love of a parent for his child. True, it is great to love one's parents, it is wonderful to love one's husband, but to love one's child is not only a noble goal, it is the culmination of the whole of life. Your faith is in our little but beautiful Czech nation. I too love this land and no matter what I may have to suffer, I mean to preserve for you and Věra this little bit of your homeland.

I shall be a friend to Pepik as I have been a friend to you. I shall see whether I deem him worthy to become your love and your friend for life.

You have understood everything that I wrote to you in my previous letter, and I too understand everything in your letter. I understand also what your hand had not written, but what your soul has imprinted between the lines. Your letter will be my charm, my talisman. I am so proud of you, so happy with you.

T hen Father wrote that he was enclosing some photographs and that only postcards were arriving from Věra, which confirmed his belief that my little sister had settled well in her new environment – seeing that she had no need to write home. Father also added that to all those who were so kind to us he could send only his endless thanks and his love and a hope that one day he may be allowed to repay them in some small measure all the kindness they were bestowing on his daughters. His letter enclosed one from Mother. Mother's letter was short, smudged a little by tears:

I too am so proud of you, I too love you with all my heart and am grateful that I am your mother. But Father said it all, his lines speak for both of us. I read and read your letter, be happy my darling. I kiss you a thousand times,
Your Mamina (Mother)

T hey trusted me so much, and thought so highly of me; I could feel the love of my parents across the land and sea. But how could I live up to their faith in me? Mixed with the joy of receiving such a letter was a sudden weight, a heaviness born out of a feeling of responsibility, not only for the kind of person I was and was to become, but for my sister and her upbringing.

Two or three letters per week arrived from home. Not knowing whether we would meet again, Mother's letters were full of love, Father's full of advice. They had so little time to impart to us all the love and wisdom they had hoped to share with us during our formative years. I remembered our Sunday walks, especially the last walk. It was my father who tried to explain to me the difficult subject of sex – a subject of which I was completely ignorant. 'Your love for a man you can express by a pressure of hand, by a kiss, by a look. Your honour is the most precious of your possessions, don't trifle with it, don't give it lightly. If temptation creeps in stop and think: Is this what I want? Is he worth it?'

I remembered Father saying that his choice was to trust people. He would rather go through life trusting his fellow travellers in this world and risk a disappointment than suspect people of ulterior motives. I knew he would not be able to use this philosophy when surrounded by the Gestapo. I so hoped Father would learn to be careful. All these thoughts I tried to put to the back of my mind. I would enjoy my holiday, I could write to my parents about my holiday. And write into my diary:

3.8.1939
We went with Suzanne and her parents to Bournemouth where there was an exhibition of Czech and Moravian handcrafts. The exhibitors were Czechs who have been in England only six weeks. I talked with them. They also feel homesick and do not know when they will be able to return home. It was a good feeling – being able to speak Czech again and knowing that I am not alone here, that there are thousands of others who, like me, believe that our country will be free again.

I had my very first swim in the sea! It was beautiful, the waves carry one, but the salt water in my eyes and nose was not very pleasant. We went to the Allners' hut by the sea; it's a wooden structure, big enough for us to change in and sit in. I think they rent it from the council or something. There are rows of these huts. Anyhow, we went on our bicycles, the boy Desmond came also. Mrs Allner, Bunty and Cedric were there. I am meeting English boys for the first time!

After the swim we had afternoon tea, played games and came home at about 7pm. I have really enjoyed myself. In the evening I wrote to Věra. Suzanne came with me to the letter box twice, as the first time I forgot to put the names of Věra's guardians on the envelope. I am writing this in my room after a bath. Suzanne's mother has just called, with a glass of milk and a goodnight kiss.

5.8.1939
Yesterday I received a wonderful letter from Mother. She writes that they were so happy to receive my card telling them of my holiday. I had returned from the sea and the letter was waiting for me.

Desmond's mother took us to the sea. We swam in the rain. I do so love to see the dark skies above the green waters of the sea on which the sailing boats rock. The seagulls look so white as they survey the scene around them. We walked on the beach and I collected shells to send to my parents and to Pepik.

6.8.1939

Today I thought so much of home; in my memories I was walking in our streets and talking with friends. I so longed to run to them all. I do believe that I shall see them again. I don't know how it can come about, it seems to me to be almost impossible for us to gain our freedom as easily as we have lost it, but in no way can I be reconciled with the thought that I will never return.

Suzanne is so happy at home, I almost envy her that her mother kisses her goodnight; I am kissed by a kind stranger. How I envied those who on our Sunday walks at school waved to their parents. If my mother and father were there I would have run to them to give them a thousand kisses. How I wish that, like others, I would be meeting my friends. They asked me here if I would be too nervous or worried to go dancing. Nothing would worry me, it seems such a little thing. I have lived through so much lately, my only happiness is the knowledge that my parents are well, that I can write to them about my joys, that I can write to Pepik about my pain as well as the joy, and that I have such nice friends there and here.

7.8.1939

The day is dawning. How I wish I were home. My poor house wins every time, wins over this big house, huge garden and much-loved ocean. Why have we lost our freedom? Whose fault was it? If we are to lose it for ever why did we earn it for twenty short years? Was it so that my generation could be born in freedom, taste its sweetness, learn to think freely and then lose it all again? To be left only with memories of a wonderful youth and childhood?

When today's youth attains adulthood, they will not allow our nation to die. We want to protect our country, be proud of it, not beg for mercy. Maybe we shall have to fight for our land. Oh, God! How many tears will be shed, how much sorrow will there be, how many unhappy people? Is there a hope for my nation without a war? Please God, give freedom back to my country. You know this prayer includes my selfish wish to return to my parents. You know how much courage is needed to be brave and not be sad. Why are You testing us all? Were we so wicked? Please forgive me if I am writing what does not please You, my thoughts are born in a broken heart, which only returning home can heal.

I received a letter from Pepik that brought back memories of the times we used to stack empty bottles in our factory. At times a thousand bottles would pass my hands, my back ached, but what fun it was! Will the time ever return? It is said that the dreams of one's youth never come back. I have the best part of my youth still in front of me, I long to share it with

26

those at home. Please God, grant us faith. Especially to my parents. My mother wrote so beautifully: 'I see my and Father's Eva – how sorrow and pain as well as hope mingle in her soul. I feel with you your sorrow, I share your hope in a better future. I too trust in God and put my faith in Him. Now I know what a treasure we have in you, I long for the time when I will be able to show you what a faithful friend your mother is to you.'

My dearest mother! It would be wonderful to be with you and Father now, after this cruel test, which has shown us how much we love each other. I put my faith in God, that He will hear and answer the prayer of all my people.

Evening
I felt so down-hearted this morning, but feel better now. Suzanne and I cooked this morning. When I was helping her to get the tennis courts ready, I stood on an ants' nest. I have never in all my life seen so many ants. In the afternoon Suzanne's friends came, among them Bunty and Cedric. I like Cedric, but I must not get fond of anyone more than I am of Pepik. We played tennis for four hours.

In the evening Suzanne's aunt showed me an article in the newspaper about our president, Beneš. He came from America to London and spoke to the Czechs who welcomed him. He emphasized his belief that truth and democracy will win, that after this crisis happy times will return. Oh, God, thank you.

8.8.1939
Today Mother sent me some photos with her letter. I replied at once, then took out half of my letter thinking that writing about President Beneš as I had done might get my parents into trouble should the letter be censored. Then I changed my mind and stuck it all back. But when I was about to post the letter I became anxious on their behalf again, and so I brought the letter home and will rewrite it tomorrow.

I feel that life has taught me to grow up so suddenly, and so I make plans for the future knowing well that fate may dispose of most of them. Yet I believe in a happy ending and I beg the Almighty to help Věra and me always to be our father's pride and our mother's joy.

I do ask myself, 'When will hatred and mankind's folly cease? When will love among men prevail?' Perhaps never, after all, I am not all that wonderful myself, how could I be pronouncing judgement on the world? The Almighty has created all, He directs it and He knows best.

B ecause of restrictions on mail imposed by the Germans, Pepik's weekly letters ceased when the war broke out in September 1939. In August in one of his final letters, he attempted to describe the changes at home:

Dearest Eva,

The situation at home here in Czechoslovakia is somewhat strange.
Yesterday we read in the newspapers of an agreement between Germany
and Russia – a non-aggression pact. I do not know if it is true, but
everybody is very surprised to hear this. I have not enough understanding
of the situation to know if this agreement is good for us or not. My limited
intelligence tells me only that hopefully now the Germans will have to
take into account what the Russians want, and I am sure that the latter
will not forget our nation and will make sure that we get back our freedom.
And then you will return again – you will come back to us – back to our
beautiful land. You have no idea how much I am looking forward to that
moment. I do hope we don't have to wait too long.

We have very little work at school. All our books are being confiscated,
examined, altered or rewritten. History is being rewritten . . . Our school
holidays are nearly upon us . . .

I include here a poem for you about our homeland, I like it very much:

MY LAND

For thousands of years I have stood here
For thousands of years I shall stand here . . .
My land, which so often was almost tortured to death:
With an inherited belief that nothing will crush you,
You who gave me all that was in your power to give,

To you I give all that is dearest to me,
Be it a mother, be it a wife, be it a lover, a daughter or a son.
This I give even if you give me bread or henbane¹ only,
Golden wheat or an empty² basket.

Through you I live, through you alone into the abyss of death can I fall.
In you transcendental beauty, you the cradle of my nation, live,
My homeland.

¹ *poisonous plant*
² *'empty' was substituted for an untranslatable word.*

My dearest Eva, I send you my greetings and hope you will have good
weather for your holidays. Yours Pepik

S even weeks after arriving in England I moved from Suzanne's
home to spend two weeks with Bunty and her family:

I thanked Suzanne's mother and everyone for having me. I have grown
fond of them during my stay, and they showed their affection for me. I am
so fortunate.

And now again I am with such kind people. The Allners' house is

smaller than the one I have left, but from the window of the room I sleep
in I can see the lake in Poole Park and the sea. What a fantastic view!
And their garden is beautiful. I seem to be accepted as part of the family
already. In the mornings I walk with Mr Allner and their sheepdog Watch
in the park and converse in my poor English. At night Mr Allner cuts a
very thin slice of bread and puts butter and Marmite on it. He divides this
into small pieces and this is Keiler's, their ginger cat's, supper . . .

Cedric and Bunty and I are spending a lot of time on Cedric's sailing
boat. I do love the sea and feel almost happy; somehow I cannot manage to
be completely happy.

Mrs Allner has allowed Bunty and me to sleep together in a huge bed. I
don't feel so alone, we talk till the early hours of the morning.

23.8.1939
We went to see something where dogs are exhibited and alloted prizes.
Beautiful dogs, all kinds of breeds, shapes and sizes. They had to sit
obediently for a long time. How much happier must be a mongrel running
freely and playing with children.

Today we spoke about the possibility of war. Senseless killing – when
mankind loses its cloak of civilization. I cannot understand how people can
behave so towards each other. I am a child. But adults don't seem to
understand any more than I do.

If a war breaks out we shall not be able to write home and letters from
home will cease. We shall be left with memories and hope.

At this time I received three cards from Father who was on
holiday. In the first card he wrote, referring to the picture on
the front of the card:

A piece of your country, a piece of your home. I have so many thoughts
but am unable to put them together in a sensible fashion. They are
confusing! In the end faith and hope prevail without a shadow. In the light
shines our happy future.
Your Táta

The next card read:

My soul, it was a beautiful day today, the weather was fantastic and
memories precious. I am sitting with a glass of beer in front of me and then
I shall go to sleep.
Your Táta

T he last card:

The valley you see on the postcard is surrounded by the mountains, Orlické Hory. Here I have spent my holiday, but today I return home. The rain caught me yesterday, I had a pleasant soaking! Thousands of kisses. Your Táta

M other had also written:

My dearest Eva,
Thank you for your letter. The photos are wonderful, you look well. Your father will return tonight, so in the meantime I can read and re-read your letter and look at your dear face to my heart's content. You can see the ocean from your window, what an unbelievable view. I almost envy the ocean for I am certain that *your* first gaze in the mornings rests on its waves as well as your last gaze at night. The windows seem to consist of little squares, something similar is used only in factories here.

I am so pleased that you write so much to Věra and that you are so helpful to her. Now you are the only one who can take care of her. Never would I have dreamt that during such tender years, when other girls of your age know only amusement, that you would be burdened with such a duty. Perhaps the Almighty will grant us the chance to make everything up to you. Both of you are so brave.

I had such a lovely letter from our Věra yesterday. It was so fantastic that I shed tears over it. And never does she forget to write that she is not homesick.

To the cats, your horse and the canary I have given your greetings and to all your friends. You write as Věra does, she also greets all the animals first and people last.

Please tell your friends that I am so very grateful to them for everything. Lots and lots of kisses,
Your Máma

I read and re-read all my letters from home so many times. Already I anticipated the isolation and the sense of loss that would be mine should a war be declared and our contact with home come to an end.

I greatly admired my new friends. There was so much love and laughter in this family. I remember my delight the first time I watched Keiler the cat curled up on Mr Allner's shoulders as he sat at the head of the table carving the 'Sunday joint' on Saturday! The rest of the meat was eaten cold on Sundays. We prepared the vegetables before going to church so that they could be cooked quickly when we returned to satisfy our hunger as fast as possible.

This family also had their worries:

The Allners are so brave: Cedric will be called up, but no one shows any fear. I love them very much. Though I am looking forward to being with my sister, I shall be sorry to leave next week. To my parents I write of my joys, but sometimes I feel guilty that I laugh when they might be sad.

L ooking back on my diaries I realize how every word, every thought, every breath of mine was affected by sorrow. Into the diaries that I hoped my parents would one day read, I poured my soul. Little did I realize what a psychologist my father was when he bid me to do so. Without this outlet I wonder how I would have survived, for normal correspondence with our home ceased with the declaration of war on 3 September 1939:

I never dreamt that one could be so lonely and go on living with this constant fear for our loved ones. The tears I shed at night do not ease my pain. Yet I was told that one feels better after a good cry. All I have is a swollen face and my heart is as heavy as it was before.

PLEASE, GOD, MAKE
THIS WAR SHORT

We were fortunate that on the day the war was declared Věra and I were together. From the time my sister and I fell into each other's arms at the station we were inseparable. I arrived in Bootle, Liverpool, on 31 August. Věra's English parents Mr and Mrs Rainford, and their daughter Dorothy, one year older than Věra, adored my sister and at once showered their affection upon me. They were poor in material things, but rich in love, which they so freely gave to two refugees. I felt drawn to them at once and grateful that their home was my sister's haven.

When three days later the declaration of war reached our ears, I recorded my mixed feelings in my diary:

Now my countrymen will have a chance to fight for their freedom. But what a price to pay. I cannot help crying for those who must fall, for those who will suffer. Oh, mankind's folly! What will happen to our parents and all those we love? Why were we chosen to escape? Will the fear in my heart ever leave me? Oh, God, protect them, hear my prayer, the whole world needs You. Please, God, make this war short, and may it bring freedom to my people. I would so like to be there, to help them.

Věra and I tried to comfort each other, we knew that our parents would be grateful for our escape to England. In our young hearts we understood that it would have been unbearable for them to have seen us suffer. Yet to know that they may suffer a fate I had escaped, filled my soul with a guilt that I could not shake off. A guilt that haunts me even now, fifty years later.

According to my poor thinking, the salvation of my nation can come only if Germany is defeated. Perhaps they are glad at home that now they have an opportunity to fight for our freedom. I would give a great deal to know what they are really thinking.

I was at the Rainford's for only a few days because Dorothy and Věra were evacuated to Southport to stay with Mr and Mrs Campion and their daughter Moyra, who is about twenty-two years old. Liverpool is thought to be too dangerous for children as it is an industrial city and will most likely be a target for German bombs.

When Mrs Campion heard our story, she insisted that I stay with my sister and added, 'Stay as long as you can and every holiday we shall be expecting you.' We have such fantastic friends.

My memory paints a picture of Mrs Campion as a very kind, talkative lady, whom I remember better than her quiet but by no means placid husband and their charming daughter Moyra. Never shall I forget their 'high teas': in the late afternoon each day the family assembled around a large table to partake of a massive meal. This started with a cooked first course, followed by a dessert plus cakes and scones. No wonder that even my skinny stature became well padded after a few meals in this household.

Mrs Campion's nephew, Desmond, became our constant companion. My diary recorded that, 'one day he put his arm around my waist, but he is very kind to Věra too'.

The days in Southport were very pleasant, in spite of our fears for those at home. Because of the uncertainty over travel caused by the war, I had to return to school a week earlier than planned and a week earlier than the rest of the pupils. I was sad to leave my new friends and heart-broken to part from my sister. It was so good to be together, share our joys, share our pain, speak Czech again, and, most of all, talk about our home. I hated leaving Věra, who was so young, so vulnerable and so brave, but I was comforted to know that she was happy and loved in her newest English home.

Alone in the dormitory I did not have much time to spare before the rest of the girls arrived a week later. Suzanne's family and the Allner family kept inviting me out, and Miss Dunn was kindness itself. I was busy writing thank you letters to Bootle and Southport and to Věra, but I feared to write to my parents in case my letters would bring them trouble. So for them I wrote my diary.

On 19 September a letter arrived from Mother. From the time war was declared any letters received were written to both Věra and me, and had to be sent to us secretly. Mother had written:

Dearest children,
I have an opportunity to send a letter and to tell you that we are well, that we think of you with hope and love and that our greatest wish is that you should be happy and full of health. We have received your letters of the 27 and 28th of last month and the one written when you were together on the 3rd of this month. The main thing is that you are well and with kind people and that you are happy. That is our comfort and joy. We too are well and never stop thinking of you, we too have faith and we also have faith in you.

At this moment Věra Hamplová is here tidying up all your things, Eva, and Marta Pavličkorá is here doing the same for Věra. What nice friends you have. I am like a captain telling them what to do.

33

It is raining a great deal, but remember if the sun does not shine and you cannot see the glitter of the stars then the raindrops bring our greetings and our love to you. And I believe you have plenty of rain in England.

Tomorrow evening Pepik will come to see us – your friends look after us. Enjoy your holiday, enjoy your school, work hard (which you do anyhow), live happily and give much love to the people around you. Give them our greetings and our thanks. Millions of kisses to you both.
From your Máma and Táta

How I wished to be what my parents wanted me to be, how I missed their guidance. We were a close, happy family, who confided in each other and who respected each other. As children we received few commands, mainly requests followed by an explanation of why we were asked to do whatever our parents wished us to do. I was not used to making decisions without discussing the pros and cons with them. In spite of all the kindness surrounding me, I felt very much alone and lived for the few letters from home.

By now our letters had to be sent to a friend of Auntie Berta who took refuge in London. His name was Robert Herczka. Věra and I were asked to write together and in German, and Mr Herczka dispatched our letters via neutral countries with the help of friends he had there. Of course, one by one most of the European countries became involved in the war. We were not permitted to write often and the diary was a poor substitute:

Dearest Mother and Father, how do you feel when you receive our letters so rarely? Are your hearts heavy and your eyes full of tears? You must be brave. As Věra wrote today, 'A soldier without faith, who is not prepared for the worst, will never win.' We too are small soldiers fighting our own battles with our consciences, our weaknesses.

1.10.1939
It is three months today since we arrived in England. Sometimes I feel that I have only just arrived, at other times that I have been here for years. How much longer will our exile last?

In her letters I feel the soul of my darling mother, feel the beat of her heart, in each unwritten line I read of her sadness. Others have survived, those at home must survive.

We must be so careful in our short letters home. I would so like to tell my parents, 'Be brave and keep smiling, Věra and I will not get lost in this world, we believe that we shall see you again.' Why are we so persecuted for the faith of our fathers? I believe in one God, the God who rules over all his people whatever their religion. I believe in His justice.

I wanted to remain faithful, I wished not to change. Not to change in adolescence? Desmond, who had driven Věra and me in his car and befriended us during my holiday in Southport, wrote to me every week. Grateful for his friendship, I would not allow myself to feel more deeply, for there was Pepik, and, more importantly, I had promised my father to stay exclusively his until my eighteenth birthday. I was haunted by a fear that I might change, that home would not be as I knew it. My natural joy and laughter were deserting me and my awareness of this was an added burden. But I was in an English boarding school, I had a chance to learn, I had to make the most of this opportunity.

Half-way through October Mrs Rainford wrote to say that Věra was in hospital with scarlet fever. In spite of my wishes I was not able to travel to see her. So I gathered together all my Czech books and sent them to her, although I knew I would not be allowed them back again because Věra was in isolation. I worried so much about my sister.

I tried not to tell my parents knowing how upset they would be, but Věra was not to write for six weeks, how could I explain this to them? So I wrote to Mr Herczka for advice. Instead of advising me, he took it upon himself to tell Mother and Father. I was furious and relieved.

There were other problems. Each Sunday all the pupils went to the Anglican church. Though baptized, in the vain hope of escaping Nazi persecution, I felt more Jewish. Should I pray our Jewish prayer or the Lord's Prayer, or carry on with both? Why were there so many religions? I had no answer, but I believed that the Almighty understood and forgave my dilemma. To my diary I confided my hope that as I grew into adulthood I too would understand.

At the end of October a short letter came from Mother and was immediately sent on to my sister.

It is such a relief when I hear from home, no matter how short the letter. Mother mentioned that she sent some money via France. Of course, this has never reached us. Anyhow, I do not need any money, both Věra and I have everything, and, should it come, I'll give it to Mr Herczka to take care of. I trust him, though I have never met him. Our parents may need the money one day.

School life continued. There were more sad faces around me as my schoolmates had fathers and brothers who were being called up. Many shed tears and I found it easy to forget my own sorrow when comforting others. Besides study, I enjoyed sport, especially hockey, which I played with joy and played well. I made a wooden box with Czech motifs for Věra – a great achievement for my clumsy hands. At this time I even ventured to write a bit of English in my diary. It was taken from one of my essays. This was the only time I veered from Czech; I must have wanted to show how much English I knew:

Why am I not at home? So many friends, so many brave Czech people are standing in their places still and fixed. No storm of the war moves them. Why I left my home, my parents and all that I love so much? It is difficult to answer. Only I know that it was the love to my parents most which said: 'You have to go. You will help your parents most if you go to England.' I could not think about this changing. I knew only it would be terrible for me to go into a foreign country to strange people . . .

No more walking in the fields, no more speaking to our work people. I was so glad if I could give pleasure to them. It was sorrowful when I gave Goodbye to all my friends, everybody said something nice, I saw everybody like me very much, I was so pleased to know it. I beseech God to give us all strength . . .

I know it was difficult for my parents to stay without weeping when they saw us in the train and said: 'We trust you. See you sometimes.' I needed all my strength to stay without tears. My parents endured and I believe we shall endure till the happy end. I believe in one God, in God which is above all people and I believe in His justice . . .

During the November half-term I was taken out by Lady Perkins, mother of my schoolfriend Nancy:

My first contact with a *real* English lady! We went in a car to Bournemouth to a Czech shop and Lady Perkins bought me a wooden mushroom for darning stockings. The Czech people in the shop gave me a Czech newspaper. I would love to buy some presents for my friends, but don't know if I have enough money. It was a lovely day.

The next day I asked Miss Dunn if it would be possible for me to order the Czech newspaper so that I could receive news in my language at regular intervals. I felt Miss Dunn was not too happy to see me, as she was busily combing her dog, but she sent me to the secretary who will arrange everything. Anyhow, I was really grateful to Lady Perkins, she was so nice to me.

Poor Nancy, she has no father, she is worse off than I am in spite of her title and money. I must add here that in the afternoon we went to see a film, though we are forbidden to do so. I have not told anyone, perhaps not telling is not lying.

After I parted from Lady Perkins, I was called to see my teacher Miss Swindles to meet her visitor who gave me chocolates. I was delighted and handed them to the matron. All the girls have chocolates and matron distributes them a little each evening – until now I had none. I still feel a stranger among the English people and don't understand all their ways, but I think they are very kind.

Desmond has written that Věra is coming out of hospital next week, hurray! I write only friendly letters to Desmond, and when I see him during

36

my next holidays I will explain that I promised my father to stay a child until I am eighteen years old. Besides, I must not fall in love in England, I must be free to return home.

Someone came to talk to us the other day, he had been to Prague, it was a pleasure to speak to him afterwards.

I had good marks this term, the lowest was sixty-four and highest ninety-five in maths. Miss Dunn asked me if I would like to be a teacher of languages. I have not thought about it, but I hope that by the time I have decided such things I will be back home.

12.11.1939
Věra is out of hospital and writes that she really enjoyed her stay there! There is a girl here, Ina, who cries so often because she is homesick. I try to comfort her, telling her she will be home in six weeks' time, that this is just one of life's tests. She says she does not feel 'at home' here and cannot understand how I can be so brave. Little does she know how my heart can ache and how much courage it takes to hold back the tears. I say to myself, 'Oh, God, please give me back the feeling of joy again.' When the sun shines and I am outside, I catch a glimpse of that joyful feeling, but it passes with the realization that I am not at home.

Today I did not feel well, and had to spend a day in bed. My head ached, I could not read, so I dreamed of home and the dreams were so real that I hated waking up.

Miss Swindles and Miss Wood often invite me into their rooms to listen to the Czech news. I do like both of them, but was so disappointed in Miss Swindles who, in front of the whole class, said to my homesick friend Ina, if she worked harder she would not be so homesick. How could she? I felt such anger in me on behalf of Ina. There is another girl here whom nobody likes. I try hard to like her because I feel sorry for her. I cannot understand why I find liking her so difficult. Perhaps some day the world will teach me.

I forgot to say that Věra instructed me to throw away her letter because she was still infectious and not allowed to write. But she is out of hospital, so I don't understand why I should do so. It was such a nice letter so I asked Mr Herczka to send it home hoping that our parents will receive it and not get scarlet fever.

I think it strange that in England one alters the clock twice a year. We do not interfere with time in Czechoslovakia. But we gained an extra hour in bed.

19.11.1939
Teaching and learning are very different here from home. I like the English way and am doing well, even though I do not understand everything. For example, we had to read a poem and then draw a picture with the poem. Yesterday we had to compose a poem of our own. We also discuss issues with our teachers and are allowed to voice our disagreement. I would not

have dared to do that at home. Today I had a letter from Věra with the news that Desmond has caught her scarlet fever. My sister asked me to write to him and added, 'and don't tell him you don't love him. Leave him the joy of loving you. That cannot do you any harm.'

Miss Dunn has arranged that I spend the Christmas holidays with Bunty, whose parents invited Věra for part of the time. Miss Dunn thinks the war will last at least three years and she hopes to meet my parents when it is all over. I read in the papers that Prague University and the high schools are being closed. The Germans will never kill the spirit of my people, we must regain our freedom. I have written to Věra that we are better off than many, but I so fear for all the dear ones at home. Have they enough food? Are they warm and safe? I cannot help them, I beg God to look after them. Faith, strength, love – will they stay with me? My contribution to the war effort is so small: some pocket money for sailors and knitting socks and scarves. We entertained small children at our school. They are evacuees from London and come from poor families and are 'distributed' among local families for the duration of the war. Poor little mites, away from their loved ones. We fed them and played with them. I am looking forward to next week when they visit us for another afternoon.

There is more news about Czechoslovakia in the papers, about persecution and death. Some people might think us lucky, might think that Věra and I have run away. No one knows how much courage it takes not to cry, not to despair at my impotence. If I was at home I would know what is happening to my parents, I would not have to await letters that do not come. I would not have to live with this constant fear of what is happening to all those I love. It is hard to be brave. I try to think of others and I pretend that my parents are watching me. I ask them, 'Is this how you wish me to behave?' I do so hope that they will be proud of me.

Every morning I meet a little robin on my way to the schoolroom. I must remember to bring him some crumbs. Yesterday I was late for my lesson, I was so busy talking to him in Czech.

My new discovery is that in England the young do not need to be the first to greet their elders. My headmaster in Czechoslovakia would have a fit if I waited for him to greet me first. Different countries, different customs.

The weather is cold; I remember looking at the frost and snow outside from the warm shelter of our home – all of us together. All that I can think of just now is, 'Are you warm, all those whom I love? Have you enough to eat?' Oh, God, please, please, protect them from all evil.

Was it cowardly to leave my country? Should I have stayed home? I must make sure that my exile will make me a better, stronger person, that I will learn a great deal so that my parents and my country can be proud of me, so that I can be of help to them when the time comes. I must remain faithful.

The fatal year of 1939 was drawing to its close. By now I understood the English language and spoke it almost fluently. My schoolmates were affectionate and thoughtful, even asking me to recite to them in Czech, knowing that to speak in my language would be of comfort to me.

We were permitted to send home only a few impersonal lines that would not reveal that we were in England. Věra sent hers to me, I added a few words and our friend, Mr Herczka, forwarded our letter through various channels known only to him to our parents. So far we had not met Mr Herczka, but I trusted him completely; after all, he was our Auntie Berta's friend. To this day I do not know which of our letters arrived at their destination. Similar messages came very infrequently from home, but I lived for them.

My attempt to hold on to 'my' faith, which I considered to be different from other people's, was strengthened by our compulsory attendance at church. I truly loved the priest when on Sunday he asked for a meeting of all who were willing to help Jews persecuted in their own countries. I had a great desire to learn about different religions:

Father used to say that to do good and to love us was his religion. I wonder what he really believes, I do wish I could talk to him. I do know that Mother has a great faith in a God of all. Miss Dunn told me today that she was pleased to see me in church and she also added, 'You are also proud to have been born Jewish, are you not?' Of course I am. Can one be a Jewish Christian? I wish I could understand more, for my and Věra's sakes.

Before Christmas we received a very short letter written by both our parents. After six months of silence Father said, 'I did not feel like writing.' Knowing this to be untrue, I was very fearful:

I do not believe this, I am sure Father was in trouble at home. It seems that everything is all right again, I just hope that they are well and holding on to their faith in a happy future – in an early reunion.

In spite of my permanent anxiety for those at home, I had a delightful Christmas. The Allners were extremely kind to me. They were a happy, well-balanced family and I shared in their joy. Amused by their eighty-year-old eccentric aunt, devoted to their eighty-three-year-old grandmother, with their cat on my lap or Watch their sheepdog at my heels, listening to Bunty playing the piano and singing, talking to their son Cedric, singing hymns by the piano on Sundays, being teased by Mr Allner who called me 'Little Girl', I felt part of a family again. And from this base, the future looked brighter, the prophesy of the school gardener who gave me flowers saying, 'Next year you will be sending me some from Prague,' seemed plausible. The Allners taught me how to dance, took me to theatres and asked me about my home. In their midst I celebrated my sixteenth birthday on 1 January 1940. In Czechoslovakia adult films were forbidden to those under sixteen and this protocol was strictly observed. My dream was to reach sixteen and go to an adult cinema:

At home, the age of sixteen years opens the gates to cinemas and dancing lessons; it is a bridge between childhood and adulthood. I always thought of this period as the nicest part of one's life. I know my parents are thinking of me, I wish I could let them know that they do not need to worry about me. But how I wish they were near, that I could ask their advice about things in life that I am encountering for the first time and know not how to deal with. The main thing is that they should be all right, should know happiness again. On the radio I heard about the persecution of Jews; I do so hope all the rumours are not true. What has happened to mankind's humanity? In spite of laughter, a silent pain has become an integral part of me, it will not leave me until a happy ending comes our way.

T he happy ending never came, and the pain remained part of my life.

Věra arrived two days later, with her sparkling blue eyes and laughing mouth and having grown in the last six months. I was so glad to have her and happy that 'my' family opened their hearts to her. I wondered what would happen if we could have returned home then. My diary witnessed my longing to be home, and my fear of how we would be seen by others; two well-fed girls set against their suffering and hunger. Yet, how gladly would I have shared all that I had. I had ten shillings from Christmas, I felt rich.

We went to dances, had a party at home and met other young people of both sexes. I talked with Bunty, and she tried to improve my clumsy dancing. When boys attempted to hold my hand I kept thinking, 'I must not fall in love, but I can be fond of someone.' What is the difference at the age of sixteen?

Then a letter came from Mr Herczka. He planned to come from London just to see us. His only request was that we find him a really warm hotel. Meeting him at the station, my first thought was, 'How could my aunt fall in love with that man?' To me he was so old (over sixty). Yet, I soon realised why:

An older gentleman, without hair, not good looking, who loves the warmth, and who is unbelievably kind. That could be his description. He has this great kindness in common with my aunt. After two days in his

40

presence I loved him too, and was really sad to see him go, and glad to darn his socks, which, he says, no one in London knows how to mend. There are no hot-water bottles to be bought, so I gave him mine. He too is alone and must be lonely.

It is lovely to have Věra here, to share our joys and sorrows, but her time is going fast. I do hope she will not be too upset when she has to leave. I find it hard to be a mother to my sister. Sometimes I think I am hard on her, but I so wish her to be a better person than I can be. And I pray that the world will be kind to her always. I feel sad today, I so miss my parents and send them all my love by the stars.

The war continued. According to the news, England was getting stronger and stronger and Germany weaker. Apparently the Germans were suffering from hunger. I was aware that my countrymen would be the first to lose their provisions to Germany. The Finns and the Russians were fighting with each other, but America talked of helping. Now we were allowed to send home only one or two lines in German via the Red Cross. I wondered whether it would not be safer for my parents if we did not write at all.

Miss Dunn invited Věra to stay in my school until the end of January, so our parting was postponed. Věra loved Sandecotes and I was so happy to have her with me. In Věra I saw myself at the age of twelve, happy and full of mischief, and at home. I searched desperately for signs of what my parents, and culture, asked of me. We both missed our parents' guiding hand, their love, their touch. There were no letters.

I was aware of the comfort my diary was to me and after a church service I wrote:

During the service we were told of the need to believe in Christ as the son of God. I keep thinking about it, but somehow cannot accept Him as equal to God. I hope that God, who is my greatest teacher, will forgive me and will help me. We recite the words, 'Who so believeth in me shall have everlasting life,' but what about those that doubt? Do my parents believe this? I would not choose everlasting life if they were not where I was to be. How can I know what happened 2000 years ago? Yet I accept as truth what is written in history books, why should I question the Bible? Perhaps in time I'll understand and have a greater faith than I have now. God will guide me, I do trust Him.

Today I have ordered a Czech magazine printed in London and have written an essay entitled, 'When I arrived in England.'

With the end of January came my parting from Věra. Both of us shed bitter tears again. Mrs Rainford travelled all the way from

Lancashire to accompany Věra home. A week later because of 'the everlasting fight between courage and despondency' (or so I wrote), I was confined to bed for a day with an aching head. I thought of those who were so much worse off than I was. I dreamt, I slept and I cried. I found a little comfort in the fact that I came first in my class in English literature and in history. This was no mean feat after only six months in England.

In February 1940, after months of silence, a short note arrived from my mother:

When I woke up this morning I felt almost free, happy. As if some of the constant sadness fell off me. I said to myself, 'What will today bring? Will it be joy or sadness again? Eva, you must believe that it will be joy, better to be an optimist than a pessimist.' So I smiled and walked to school and on the way I was handed twenty-five words, written by our mother, to tell me that they had received thirty (I wrote two pages) words from me and that they are well and brave. I only hope that it is true. Mother would not tell me, for fear of worrying me unnecessarily, if things were wrong. I cannot but worry about Father, why did he not write? When I read in the papers what is happening to Jews under the Nazis I am near to despair. All I can do is to beg You, God Almighty, to take care of them.

This very civilized England is a quaint country, where many strange customs still persist. On 14 February was 'St Valentine's Day'. Those in love send secret letters to each other. And six weeks before Easter Day, they have 'Shrove Tuesday' and make and eat pancakes. On St Agnes' Eve (6 January), girls and boys go to bed without supper. On their way to bed they must not look right nor left and must walk in the dark in order to dream about the one they will marry.

I am making a picture frame for Věra. Also I have composed a Czech poem, full of hope. Faith, love and hope must be our motto.

I talk with Mr Jones, the gardener, each day. Today he said that this time next year I shall be home. It seems like a fairy tale. I look at the moon and the stars from the window by my bed, and dream of the reality of this tale.

A s February 1940 drew to its close, a letter arrived from Auntie Berta. This one came via Holland and was written in Czech. It was to be our last letter in Czech. Auntie Berta's letter confirmed that our relatives received some of our messages from Christmas, when Věra and I were together, for Auntie had written:

Dear Children!
We were all very happy when we heard that you were together and that you spent at least part of your holidays in each other's company. Also, we

were very pleased that Robert Herczka visited you and that he was so good to you. It is wonderful that your school reports were so good. We sing your praises, we know that neither of you will ever disappoint us. We laughed at the thought of Věra at school performing as a cat with glasses! We were also pleased that you received so many gifts. It is wonderful for us to know that you are happy and are enjoying life.

Please write again soon, but do not number your letters, we receive them all. All of us are well, we think of you all the time with great joy. Irma and her husband are here once or twice a week, which always cheers us up. They send their greetings and kiss you both a thousand times . . .

The winter here was very cold, everyone walked about wrapped up in shawls, and women looked like real old grannies. Only the young looked wonderful, but everything is becoming on the young – you too would look pretty no matter what you wore. Please give our greetings to Robert. I am sure he disappointed you in his appearance, but that should not matter as he is very kind and will always advise you to the best of his ability. We are glad to hear you are putting on weight, but at the same time we hope your dresses still fit you so that your friends do not have too many expenses. Please give them all our best wishes, and all of us kiss you both affectionately.

Yours Berta

I did wonder why Auntie called Mother 'Irma' and why my parents did not add to the letter. But to have news during these days of uncertainty was enough. And this was a *real* letter. After all, by 1940 news from home was scarce and consisted of a few words only.

It was a cold winter for England. We were told to stay indoors by the fire. My longing for fresh air compelled me to break the rules and go for forbidden runs in the large grounds surrounding us. It was an honour to be asked to walk at night with the mistress responsible for 'lights'; I could stare at the bright stars and shining moon without a window between us. Having ascertained that no flicker of light could be visible to the German planes from above, I returned to the dormitory.

My patience was often taxed by various occurrences in the dormitory or classroom, but I curbed my inclination to argue, thinking that to be silent was 'the English way'. Instead I studied, tried to practise on the piano and enjoyed the sport, especially hockey. I was interested in everything, at least for the duration of study.

Věra was so pleased with the wooden box I made for her. And *Czechoslovak*, the Czech magazine printed in London, has arrived. Other refugees are writing in it. I know I am not alone, not the only one far from home.

Today we went by bus to the sea. My heart feels almost light, and when my heart is light my legs move faster and so do my fingers, so that even playing the piano was a pleasurable exercise today. I write nothing about the war in my diary, history will tell better than I can what is going on. My diary will tell my parents only of my experiences in England. It will be a book into which serious and foolish things are written. Perhaps much is repetitive; yet this diary contains part of the soul of sixteen-year-old Eva and her memories. And what else is our past, what else but memories?

N ow and then I had the opportunity to send a few lines to my parents. That I could write no more than those few words was painful, but it did not worry me as much as the fear that even these might harm my parents. Would they prefer the few lines, and the risk, or would they prefer not to hear at all? I felt that the first choice would be theirs, and prayed that no action of mine, however well meant, would put them in danger.

Czech, English and German books were keeping me busy, as well as homework. On 3 March 1940 our half-term began and I spent that day with the Allners:

Mrs Allner came for me in the car, and I was content to stand in front of their fireplace, rest my head on the mantelpiece and watch the flames. It seemed to me that they were jumping for joy. Yet even the flames change. Nothing is without a change, only the One who is the highest, the One who is above all of us, who is everlasting yet unknown, a father and ruler of all, the One we call God. Our love for Him helps us to be better human beings.

Mr Allner was sick, so he did not go with us for a picnic into the country. Blue Lake was frozen, the countryside looked beautiful and I ran across the fields and hills and felt like a bird released from its cage, tasting freedom. The humming of the trees, warmth of the sunrays and songs of the birds made me feel light, just for a little while, for I tried not to think of home. I remembered writing in my diary, when I was thirteen years old, 'I feel so happy, so very happy, that I fear such joy cannot last.' It did not. Will I ever be so happy, so carefree again?

I was surprised that our composer Smetana was less well known in England than Dvořak, but my music teacher played 'Má Vlast' and 'Vltava' for me as my own piano playing left much to be desired. Patriotic as always, I thought of our first president, Thomas Masaryk, on 7 March, his birthday, and remembered his motto that 'Truth will prevail'. The month of March also brought Aunt Berta's birthday and the last day of March my mother's birthday:

God give me strength to remain true to the promise I gave my parents. I cannot kiss my mother on her birthday and am unable to give her a present for which I would be saving the whole year, as I did at home. My heart, my love, my longings, these belong to my parents always. They had my love from the first moment of my understanding, maybe from the moment when as a babe I whispered 'máma'. The word 'máma' (mother) is the dearest word I know, in it is contained all the love a child's heart is capable of. Věra does not understand this, she is still a child and I want to be of help to her, to advise her – so that she does not miss you quite so much. I have to face life, reality, without your guiding hand.

Today, in church, the sermon was about Jews, that even for them it is possible to love Christ. That love may help them to shed their hatred of the Germans when the war is over, and not only Jews, but all the oppressed nations will have to learn to love again – and to forgive. Yet I do not believe that only hatred is pervading the hearts of those at home, they also feel love for their country and for each other. I can only feel what 'love' means, truly Christian love, but cannot quite understand it. But can one ever understand *love*? It is such a wonderful, magical overpowering feeling. Maybe if one thought about it too much it would lose its worth. I would like to understand religion more, in the meantime I trust in a God of all peoples. Each one of us has his own faith.

I had chilblains on my hands that were painful and bleeding. I was losing weight through worry, no letters arrived from home and fear for my parents seemed intolerable. I could not sleep. I did not share my constant fear for my parents and relatives with anyone. I longed for newspapers that discussed the problems in Czechoslovakia. I managed to pay for the one printed in London called *Czechoslovak*, but I did not have enough money for *Československý Boj*, printed in France. My history teacher, upon discovering this, declared that the latter was what she wished to read (the English edition). The kind lady subscribed to it and gave me the editions as soon as she finished with them. I did not appreciate this hidden kindness until years later.

In her sermon, the headmistress stressed the need to pray in church, not in the country, and I turned to my God for His understanding:

I feel closest to God among the birds and flowers under the blue sky, where the humming of bees accompanies my prayers. Even at home my bicycle used to carry me far from civilization, towards the river that was twisting and turning among the fields, whenever my heart was sad or full of joy.

A very short message came from Father just before Easter. He wrote to say they were well and not to worry about them. That was all. The letter was written in German and it was dispatched at once to Věra for her to share my joy:

I feel so happy. I have told everyone. I could not contain myself. And when on a short walk my form mistress put her arm around me my joy was complete. I never realized how much I missed the human touch pervading our family but so lacking in my life in England. And a friend gave me a bunch of violets, my father's favourite flower! I could have kissed her but did not dare! England is beautiful in spring time.

MY SISTER — MY JOY
AND MY BURDEN

A pril 1940 was almost gone and with it our school term. My school report was excellent, I even came first in many subjects. In my diary I questioned whether I deserved this. I so longed to be able to share my pleasure with my parents. I felt I did not let them down.

My sister's English family had moved from Bootle in Liverpool to Ainsdale. Living further from Liverpool they hoped to escape the persistent bombing. Věra and Dorothy were therefore able to gravitate between the Rainfords and Campions. I spent my Easter holiday with Věra in Ainsdale, delighted to be with my sister and conscious of the Rainfords' love for us both. Indeed, we had much to be grateful for. Ainsdale in Lancashire was near the sea. The magnificent sand dunes called me each morning. After the restrictions at school, I felt as free as a bird and did not care if anyone saw me running and singing, making somersaults and cartwheels, before Věra and I returned to tidy our bedroom and our hosts' living-room. I was also permitted to use Dorothy's bicycle in order to explore the countryside with my sister:

The Rainfords' kindness shines out of their eyes. Mr Rainford is so tall and his wife quite short and their only daughter Dorothy shows no jealousy towards Věra. But I was really furious when I discovered that Věra tells lies, what would our parents say? She is young and full of life, but she can be very naughty. I suppose at the age of twelve she is only a child and must be naughty sometimes.

I was very worried when Věra caught flu. Fortunately, she recovered quickly.

Again Desmond was our companion for much of the time. I knew he was still in love with me. Faithful to my promise to my father not to fall in love until I was eighteen years old, I held tightly on to my heart. In retrospect, that denial of my own feelings made it, for much of my life, harder for me to understand those feelings, and harder when I was aware of them to follow my heart.

Věra and I went to church as was expected of us, went for picnics, walked and cycled and talked and talked, especially when alone, for then we could converse in Czech. I truly enjoyed my holiday.

In the meantime the Battle of Britain continued. This included indiscriminate bombing by the Luftwaffe of residential centres, especially in London. Both sides incurred great losses, but Hitler failed to get superiority. The sky above London belonged to the RAF. The Germans concentrated on night bombing:

Are we supposed to be civilized human beings, dropping bombs on innocent victims? The English suffer and so do the German people on whom our bombs fall. Is fighting the only way human beings have to sort out their differences? Is this the only way to gain back our freedom? This is hard to understand.

Our friend Mr Herczka has written and confirmed my fears that normal letters home will have to cease. Only now and then shall we be allowed to send a few words. He also begged me to spend a couple of days in London on my way back to school because he was lonely and had little money to travel himself. I knew I had to ask Miss Dunn's permission to do so. The permission was not granted because of the German onslaught and so I shall travel directly to Bournemouth. As for Desmond, it is hard to let my head rule my heart when my whole being seems to cry with the need to love and be loved. To disobey my parents when they were near and would chastise me was one thing. But to disobey them when they are far, when I cannot explain, when they might be suffering, when they are trusting me, I cannot do that at any price. I never want to let you down, my dearest Mother and Father, but sometimes I wonder if what I am doing is what you really would wish me to do. The main thing is that you should be all right. Please, God, look after them.

I was grateful to Desmond for his affection and well aware how easy it would have been to return it in full measure.

I appreciated the physical freedom I had during these holidays beyond all measure. My prayers to the Almighty soared from my heart when enveloped by the beauty of nature. I was well aware of the love of the two families who were taking care of my sister. I was truly grateful, especially on Věra's behalf. My 'home' in England was a boarding school that was, by my standards, very posh; yet how much more fortunate was my sister. I was indeed lucky to be able to share my holidays with her.

We both cried bitter tears when parting. With each separation, with each packing, I suffered the same anguish as when I left my home. I was glad to know that Věra recovered more quickly. To her I hoped to impart the wisdom I felt our parents wanted her to have. But from whence would I seek it for myself? I confided everything to my diary:

Desmond understood when he said, 'At home you would have copied your parents, but here?'

'Here I have to try to do what I feel they would wish,' I answered.

As I had to change trains in London and had a few hours to spare, Mr Herczka met me at the station and bought me some Czech food and sweets. He could not understand why I felt I had to obey Miss Dunn and not prolong my stay with him. To me he seemes to have grown older; he is still so kind, I do wish I could do something to ease his life.

I n May 1940 Winston Churchill became Prime Minister of England, replacing Neville Chamberlain:

Will he be able to finish the war quickly?

I have been given a new tennis racket and my playing has improved greatly. I do love the fresh air – the wind in my hair, the sun on my face. My parents used to call me 'a child of nature with laughing brown eyes'. Now my eyes probably reflect the pain that I wish to hide from others.

T he pain grew greater when I received an unexpected letter from home with an enclosed one for Mr Herczka. This letter came via Holland – the last one that Mr Herczka's Dutch friend was able to forward:

Father's short letter was written in German asking us to send only a line and in German if an opportunity came our way, as he had difficulties with the authorities because of what we had written. But Father stressed that they were all right and that all was well at home.

I did not believe him and so I did something I am rather ashamed of – except that I simply had to know the truth. I opened the letter meant for Mr Herczka written to him by our Auntie Berta. In it I read of their fears, of the uncertainties at home, that Father was about to have his business taken away, that curfew prohibited their going out in the dark. Each knock on the door spelt terror in their hearts – will they be the next to be taken away to concentration camps?

My dearest parents, I am so fearful for you, I love you so much, please, God, please, protect them all. I keep thinking of you, I wish so much that I could help you in whatever hardships you have to face. I know that the joy I felt during these past holidays would gladden your hearts, yet I feel so guilty that I laughed when you have suffered.

A t school we were given gasmasks, and long dark shelters appeared in the grounds.

May 1940

The Germans have overrun Holland, and with it is disappearing our last route for communication with our parents. Perhaps we can write through the Red Cross. In the stillness of the night we can dimly hear the Dutch guns – will Belgium be next on the list?

One teacher lent me *Democracy Today and Tomorrow* written by our president, Beneš. I find it hard to follow, but I struggle through and try to understand as much as I can.

At night I dream of home; not always, but very often . . .

The Germans have turned their armies towards France. England has celebrated a 'Day of National Prayer' (perhaps I should not say celebrated) and I went with my school to church. I tried to follow the sermon and the prayers, and longed for greater understanding and greater faith. My mother used to say, 'What God does, He does well and nothing happens without His will.' I wonder what He thinks about all the destructive forces in this world.

I n spite of study, in spite of excellent marks and having an article published in the *School Chronicle*, in spite of great kindness showered on me by my schoolmates and teachers, my eyes were full of tears far too often, for I could do nothing to help those at home. I lost so much weight that I looked like a skeleton. Then Belgium fell.

President Beneš was now in London and I wrote a letter to him to show my appreciation for all that he was doing for our country. I was thrilled when his answer came, written and signed by him. 'Be a good student, you will soon be home,' was the theme of his letter. During my stay in England I wrote twice more to our president and each time he answered. The three letters signed by him are amongst my greatest treasures.

Having reached the age of sixteen I had to report to the police every time I slept away from my school. I was a 'friendly' alien, and the policemen became my friends through frequent interaction.

France fell to the Germans in June 1940, and our French mistress entertained to tea many soldiers who participated at Dunkirk. About 338,000 troops were rescued from the beaches of Dunkirk. I was very proud of these fighters against oppression.

Then Italy declared war on England. In my diary I wrote:

Hitler prophesized that in June he will be in Paris and in August in London. Is it possible? Our maid Emča (she refused to leave us to marry her boyfriend) feared that a war could spell the end of the world. Could she be right? I hope not.

There is a blackout in England, no lights are allowed to show anywhere in the night. One is not permitted to light as much as a matchstick. And again we can hear the guns – probably from across the Channel.

My dearest parents, are you brave? How are you? Fear for you makes my whole body so tight, I cannot eat and I keep getting lectures that I must eat more, for I weigh only six stone and look awful.

Whenever I can I spend time with Jones the gardener, he is sure we shall not lose the war. Sometimes I think he is more worried about the weather and how the lack of rain will affect his garden. Oh dear, I so wish I could do something to help in the war effort; I am studying really hard and learning much and getting high marks, but is that enough?

Mr Churchill spoke on the radio telling us to be courageous and not to spread panic. My little sister wrote, she too is worried. In my reply to her I tried to give comfort, strength and hope.

I n June 1940 we had the first air-raid on Poole's naval dockyards, only about five miles from our school:

... We heard the siren, and the school bell rang. As instructed, we put on our coats and took our gasmasks, and one by one went into the narrow, dark and stuffy air-raid shelter built underground. Three girls felt ill and had to be taken out, the rest of us sang for nearly four hours before the all-clear went. I was not in the least afraid, but was glad of the extra hour's sleep allowed us this morning. We were to rest after lunch, but I could not sleep, so I thought of home. Will I ever see my grandparents again? I love them so much, they were so easy to talk to and so wise. My grandfather recited poetry, was a great musician and a good businessman. I loved to sit on his lap and listen to his talk whilst his grey beard tickled my chin. And as for our blind grandmother – her cooking and her stories were the delight of my childhood. She knew her large flat and kitchen like the palm of her hand; if one did not perceive her unseeing eyes one would not be aware of her blindness. How would she manage if they had to move?

M any girls left school as their parents were leaving either for the country or for a safer land such as Canada or Australia. Tears were shed and bonds of friendship offered. Knowing what parting meant, I tried to comfort others. I kept my tears for the few letters I re-read with a torch, under the bedclothes at night. There I also continued my studies until apprehended by a school mistress.

We were permitted to spend three days per term out of school, and my friends, the Allners, allowed me to share in their family circle. They, too, had their fears, for their son Cedric went from Oxford to the army. His sailing boat was entrusted to my care, as I was the only 'member' of the family who truly loved the freedom of the ocean.

We had air-raids almost daily. The Allners had put a brick wall outside the windows of a downstairs room and this was their shelter. The dog Watch and cat Keiler ran there at the first sign of enemy planes, which they seemed to have heard even before the siren went.

Whilst others were told to work harder, I was begged not to study so much. My eyes were swollen, my head hurt. In those days I greatly admired our headmistress, who never showed any fear nor her tiredness; yet I knew she slept by the telephone and took her responsibility for us all very seriously. Over forty girls left that term, some gladly, some were very sad. Margaret, three years my junior, sat one night on my bed and cried because of homesickness:

Margaret said that I am brave because I am older. Little does she know! She argued that one never knows of the bad things that could happen. I told her that one does not know about the good things lying ahead of us, and that, for all she knows, she might soon go home. She said, 'That will never happen,' and yet, a few days later her family came for her. How could I not believe in You, God, in everything You demonstrate, how very strange are Your ways.

Most of the Czech soldiers and airmen fighting in France have managed to escape to England, according to an article in *The Times*. I am so proud of my Czech countrymen. This little island now stands alone against the might of the German armies.

Before the exams, I walked into a room where the exam questions were lying on the desk. I never knew that the temptation to look and thus cheat could be so strong. I had to run out of the room! I was glad, for my results were excellent without cheating. The photos of my parents were in front of me as I wrote, on my neck I wore the little cross they gave me and my tiny elephant that I used to wear at home for luck. I do so want to be worthy of my parents. Will they think me worthy to be their daughter? They would have been so sad that they could not write for Věra's twelfth birthday. I did try to make it up to her and wrote that they could not send their most precious gift for it is embedded deeply in their hearts.

As our school was in a defence area and because so many pupils had left, the church council, to whom the school belonged and who owned two other schools, decided to close Sandecotes at the end of the school year. Our headmistress and many others were to lose their jobs. I did not worry that I would have nowhere to go, I was prepared to work for my living. Fearing that Miss Dunn might be concerned on my behalf, I went to tell her that I would be all right – and then I learned from her that the school council was responsible for me, not her. I felt somehow cheated. Not used to charity, the need to thank and to know who the provider was seemed important.

I felt so sorry for all those who would be without their jobs, especially my friends the gardener and the waiter who used to remove my full plate when I winked at him. Having grown fond of everyone and feeling part of a school family, I faced another parting and shed bitter tears with the rest of the girls.

I longed to accept Mrs Allner's invitation to share their home and go to a day school. However, my future was not in my hands; it was decided by the council that I was to go to Uplands, a sister school evacuated from Hastings to Monmouth in Wales:

At least I can study for another year. Just now I am reading like mad, both in English and German. The mistresses are lending me their books. During reading I am transported to other lands, other cultures, suffer other people's pain and share in their joy. Thus I forget my own hidden pain, which never leaves me.

I had such a good school report, everyone congratulated me, my parents would be proud of me. Strangely, I really love learning, it is no effort, more like a voyage of discovery. But I shall be sorry to leave this school, the friends I have made, the now familiar countryside where I chase wind on my bicycle.

I spent the first part of my summer holiday in 1940 with the Allner family. I was content in their midst, for they treated me like one of them. I was to see Věra in September. She wrote that she was having a happy holiday with her family. I was glad, but perplexed and angry when I heard from Mr Herczka that Věra demanded a tennis racket from him in spite of my asking her not to do so. Mr Herczka was hurt mainly because she never thanked him for it:

I am very angry with Věra. I wrote and said that she is not to forget her duties, even though she is surrounded by pleasures. Mother and Father, how shall I bring up my sister when I do not know how to bring up myself? I do need your advice. I listen to the radio and hear the lies the Germans are telling you, I do hope you don't believe them. I cry for you, you must believe that we shall be victorious.

There was hardly a day when we did not hear sirens sending us into shelters. The Germans also dropped leaflets printed with Hitler's speeches. These were welcome, not for the speech, but because there was a shortage of paper. The indomitable British spirit manifested itself on bombed-out houses that carried such notices as, 'Business as usual'. And business as usual it was.

On Sundays we sang hymns, Mr Allner playing the piano. Granny always chose the hymn for those absent. We remembered Cedric now in the army, and I thought of all those at home and wished them courage. I wrote in my diary that, 'In the midst of this family I see the future as bright.' I also noted how happy I was when one night Mrs Allner kissed me, for she was not a demonstrative person. Again I realized how much I missed physical contact with my parents, as kissing and cuddling was a daily menu in our family.

Bunty and I were growing up, and unexpected frictions arose between us that neither of us understood and both of us were sorry for afterwards:

15.8.1940

Bunty is sorry when I am sad, and says that she cannot understand herself and feels changed, and not as happy as she used to be. The war is changing all of us. Everyone has to make sacrifices; as there is no building going on, Mr Allner, an architect, has little work. Their beach hut has been confiscated, and we have to be careful with food. But no one is complaining, everyone agrees that these precautions are necessary to win the war. The war: it spells hatred, killing, blood. I remember seeing fighting in the cinema at home; I used to shut my eyes and could not accept that man would behave like this. I used to shake with anger and pain, asking, 'Is this real life? The life I do not know?' And now, the real life is here, it has knocked on my door and entered – and I have to live it. Gone is the complete happiness I once knew. Whatever the future holds it will never return, my laughter will always be tinged with sadness.

Each day we have air-raids. Yesterday we watched a German parachutist jump into the harbour, but our boys rescued him. So many of the enemy planes fly over our heads and somehow none of us is afraid. We shot down 555 German planes as opposed to 134 of ours. What cruelty, so many lives lost. Hitler said that today he will be in England. On the radio someone remarked that a place in the concert hall is reserved for him. How strange the English are, and how I love them. I shall miss Mr Allner and our morning walks and evening talks in the garden. He is so kind and wise.

The bombs did much damage: in my diary I wrote about an old lady who was furious with Hitler because, 'He dared to damage my house.' I, too, was angry, because the noise from the German planes stifled the sound of the waves that sung their lullaby as I fell asleep.

At the beginning of September I was to spend a fortnight with my sister, however, because of air-raids and difficulties in changing stations, Mrs Allner and Věra's guardian thought it better for me to stay where I was. I wished to stay, yet in my ears rang my Father's voice, 'Look after Věra,' and before me I saw my sister's blue eyes full of tears. 'And her eyes must be full of laughter,' I wrote in my diary. And so I begged that I be allowed to go. My kind family took it upon themselves to help. Mr Allner travelled with me to London to take me to the right station and to put me on the right train:

I felt so much love for this good person, it was not just gratefulness. I am often afraid that I could mix up sorrow and gratefulness for love. Of pity I have the same feeling, if people like me I hope it is because I am me, not that they feel sorry for me.

I went rowing on the river with Bunty the day before I left, and the inevitable siren went. So we sat under trees eating our sandwiches and watching German planes over our heads. As the all-clear did not go for a long time we had a swim – and then went on rowing somewhat to the consternation of English soldiers who were near by. At night there was another raid, yet the English take it all in their stride, and so do I.

3.9.1940
I arrived safely in Liverpool, where I was met by Mrs Rainford and taken to their home in Ainsdale, where Věra and I fell into each other's arms. The next day we went to visit Czech soldiers in a hospital in Liverpool. They were so pleased to see young Czech girls. On our way back the siren went. We had to go to the shelter and arrived home an hour later than expected. Mrs Rainford was very worried, and from now on we keep in touch with our sick countrymen by correspondence. We are forbidden to go to Liverpool.

T he happy time with my sister went far too quickly and on 17 September 1940 I left her and her family to face yet another life at Upland School, evacuated from Hastings to Lady Rose's Estate, 'The Hendre', in Monmouth.

LIFE SEEMS LESS PERPLEXING

The magnificent home that housed our school was huge, cold and draughty, but it stood in the midst of the most beautiful countryside, with green fields, rolling hills and woods that feasted our gaze as far as we could see. I made new friends; this time all the pupils were boarders with parents in other parts of England. I received encouraging letters from Miss Dunn and the Allners that helped me to settle in my new surroundings.

Each Sunday we walk two miles to a little church in the country, I think there is a great difference between the well-to-do parishioners of my previous church and those surrounding me now. The latter seem to be closer to the Czech people in the village I had to leave.

Some of the girls meet boys from the nearby high school, I too am tempted. It is forbidden, should I obey? I don't wish to disappoint you, Mother and Father, but there is a great difference between obedience and having fun, and they do not seem to be compatible at times. It seems to me that I am far too serious and any time I make the slightest mistake I think of myself as bad.

With other girls I visited the country folk on foot or on Miss Dunn's old bicycle, which was much in use. I read profusely, perhaps too much, as even Miss Dunn reprimanded me in her letters for working too hard and asked me to have fun and to laugh. Soon it was November:

Mr Chamberlain has died – having finished his task. Perhaps he helped England by giving her an extra year of peace, but that decision has increased the suffering of other people. The future will show what was right, life is such a puzzle. I suppose Mr Chamberlain made what he considered to be the right decision when he sacrificed my country for the sake of peace in 1938.

Today is 11 November and my father's birthday. I am wearing my best dress and am thinking of him all the time. Without love and without friends life would be too cruel.

56

12.11.1940

After almost six months of silence we have received a very short note written in German from Mother. They are alive and sound all right! I have told everyone and wrote to all my friends and the girls from Sandecotes, nearly all my money has been spent on stamps. Of course, the first letter went to my sister, she will be so thrilled. How the note was sent I do not know.

Mother has written: 'It is Sunday, we are with your grandparents and as always are thinking of you. We know, and this is of comfort to us, that you are well, brave and working hard. We are well, nothing new, our best wishes and kisses Irma.' To hear that all is well is enough.

I also had a letter from a friend I knew at Sandecotes, she is not very happy in her new school. We correspond a great deal. She calls me her Czech mother with sparkling diamond eyes. Funny girl, I am glad my letters cheer her up.

I was looking forward to the forthcoming Christmas holiday that Věra and I were to spend with Bunty and her parents:

I feel their warmth, I feel part of this family. Because Mr Allner calls me 'Little Girl' I call him 'Big Man'.

Whenever I think about the present war it seems to me that I have read of similar situations in history books. Does mankind never learn? Yet this war seems even more cruel – perhaps it is so because it touches me. I am also learning about religion. That is hard, but I want to understand. I remember Father saying once that mankind believes because our nature is weak and we need a power that would help us to be and do good. It seems to me that no one is so strong that they can walk through life without some faith. I know that it helps. And the Bible? It is the oldest history book, and Christ was love, an example to us all. I wish I could discuss these things, but there is no one and the girls here don't seem to understand any more than I do.

Towards the end of 1940, English cities suffered from much bombing, Coventry especially; already in September there had been a funeral for over 170 victims. In our country retreat we escaped this; there was no more running into shelters for me. In my new school, learning and study were again my priority, but relaxation was there as well. I especially enjoyed activities out of doors, such as 'hare and hounds', when we ran over lanes and fields and hills, chasing each other often for three to four hours, regardless of mud and streams. Then I was able to disregard toes sore from chilblains and was proud to be one of the first to return to our destination.

The frequent 'house parties' were also fun, the food served there was luxurious compared to our daily menu, and we made the most of it. I participated in various plays and enjoyed the challenge. Life seemed freer than in Sandecotes; even in our dormitories the girls who surreptitiously remade our beds so that we could not get in went unpunished. As all of us were far from home, visits from parents were infrequent and our teachers attempted to provide us with a home environment. I often fell asleep feeling content with my life, attempting to push into the background my fear for those at home. Boasting of an excellent school report, I was happy on my parents' behalf:

I love learning, and when I study history, I feel I understand so much more than last year, life does not seem to be quite so perplexing. I think I know what our parents meant by the word 'anxiety' and 'politics'. I am reading *The Case of Federal Union* by W. B. Curry, it is difficult but I do enjoy the search for understanding. I am in a foreign land on trial, and this experience is teaching me a lot, though it has taken a lot away from me too. In some ways, I would lack much of my knowledge had I not come to England. And now I am nearly seventeen years old with a heart crying for love – at home it would be for boys, here it is for the love of my parents. Yet I know I have it no matter where they are. I think of you my dearest ones with each dawn and with each sunset, may God bless you and give you courage.

I could hardly wait for 19 December when, on my way to Parkstone, I met my sister and we travelled together:

Poor Bunty and Big Man, they waited over three hours at the station because the train was late. I was so very happy to see them all again. I am so very fond of them, and I know that my feeling is reciprocated. I have a pretty sister and was somewhat glad to hear Bunty's uncle say that he thinks me very pretty too, but wishes me not to be so thin! I do love Věra and am so happy to have her here, but she is old enough now not to constantly cheat at games and tell lies. How can I help her, prevent her doing this?

On my seventeenth birthday on New Year's Day 1941, in spite of the gifts and kind wishes and a very welcome letter from Cedric – who wanted to send me cod-liver oil to increase my weight – I thought of all those at home. I wished I could send them some of the food we had; I imagined my mother with a tear-stained face; saw Father's head resting on the table as was his want when worried; and thought of my grandparents and other relatives, of my friends, so many of them, so far away. Would we ever meet again? Would we understand each other if we did meet? I was aware that the experiences fashioning my life differed greatly from the lives they were leading.

In spite of the hidden sorrow, Věra and I enjoyed every moment of our holiday in my friends' delightful home. One day I confessed to Mr Allner that I thought the English to be masters at hiding their feelings. In my diary is written his reply:

'We try to find something funny in everything, that is why we like jokes. Like the one about the Italians who are now fighting on the side of the Germans. We say that in the last war we had to put up with them and now it is time that the Germans suffered the same fate!'

E nglish jokes! I was beginning to grasp what it meant to be English when I could laugh at the jokes in *Punch* – the most English magazine (so I thought).

And thus came the end of our holiday. A few days after my return to school a letter from Auntie Berta found its way to us:

Auntie says not to worry, that all is well at home and that they are strengthened by the knowledge that we are brave and will not disappoint them. My fear is that with the best intention I might be guilty of an action of which my parents would disapprove.

M iss Vinall continued to return my letters corrected with red ink, as did Miss Dunsby, who taught me German at Sandecotes. I appreciated their encouraging remarks greatly. However, the winter term, with frost, snow and dampness, helped to decrease my resistance. The chilblains on my feet were large and sore and prevented me from participating in outdoor sport. I was bitterly disappointed. I was also afraid as my menstruation ceased. Not confiding in anyone and not understanding that this was the result of my thinness and general state of health, I lived in fear that I would be unable to bear children. If I knew anything at all, I knew that I hoped to have children and be part of a loving family.

One day, as I was washing, my gold chain with the little cross from home broke, and fell down the basin:

All the girls helped me to search for it. I imagined it flowing down the pipes into streams and rivers. I almost cried myself to sleep, but I was woken up early by one of the girls who went on searching after I gave up. She had found my chain and cross caught under the drain of the basin. To feel as happy as I do now was almost worth the sorrow I felt last night. The girls are so caring.

This caring was demonstrated in various ways. When the Czech national anthem was played on the radio everyone stood up. During dancing lessons our teacher, Miss Cole, taught us Czech dances. Whenever my country was mentioned in the newspapers, the girls or the teachers brought this to my attention. It was my privilege to be permitted to listen at night to Czech news from Britain. This was broadcasted to Europe to those brave enough to defy the Nazis and listen in secret. Thus I learnt of the persecution of Jews in my country, that a yellow star was to be their identification wherever they went. I learnt of their confinement to their houses at night, of punishment for befriending them. I heard that Jewish children were forbidden to go to school, and I thought sadly of our two cousins, Honza and Tomíček, who missed the last transport to England. I hoped Věra was not worried by this news. I tried not to show my great fear and anxiety for our parents in my letters to her. Each week I wrote to my sister and to 'my' family, the Allners. Their home was my anchor. Here is part of a letter from Mr Allner, my 'Big Man':

My dear Little Girl,
We have to say thank you for two letters this time. We are always so glad to hear from you and look forward to hearing how you are faring . . .
I am interested to read that Mr Churchill never liked Latin – and in that way only feel almost his equal myself. I could never get on with it (and often say I know of at least 2000 hours of my life that could have been spent more profitably). All the same, I suppose it is good to have struggled with a little of it – a very little.
I should think making toast for eighteen would be almost enough to make you tired of it.
I am glad you enjoyed reading *Westward Ho* and I have thought of another book which I believe you would like if you have not already read it. It is called *Ben Hur*. Let me know if you have not yet read it and I'll try and find you a copy . . .
Although there is little building going on in the ordinary way I get lots of odds and ends that keep me busy . . .
Will enclose a cutting from the paper which will probably amuse you. A subaltern is a junior army officer (below the rank of captain). With dear love from us all, Little Girl.

The enclosed cutting read:

This is a story of a subaltern who was woken up the night before Bardia with the news that 500 Italians wanted to surrender.

'Tell them they cannot,' he said sleepily. 'The battle isn't till tomorrow. Tell them to come again later.'

O n 15 March 1941 I chose a quiet spot in the study to sit and remember. Remember that precisely two years ago the German army marched into my homeland, my mother lost her laughter, and the wrinkles on my father's face increased. My Czech school was partly occupied, people spoke in whispers. Sadness and fear – until then unknown to me – pervaded our world. I thought of all the loved ones at home, and prayed to the Almighty to give them courage. And I thought of my mother on 31 March, her birthday, remembering how I used to save my pocket money for months in order to buy her a present. I wished her health and happiness, I wished her courage. By the moon and the stars my thoughts travelled to her. In my heart I felt that the dearest mother in all the world felt my longing, knew of my wishes for her.

The end of the winter term arrived. I came second in the class, enjoyed my achievement and enjoyed the end-of-term celebrations. The last sermon for the term in the little village church made a great impression on me:

The cross is the symbol of Christians, it signifies that Christ rose from the dead. That is what the priest was saying. Further he said that many people do not believe that Christ has risen from the dead, and if it were not true then Christian faith would be just an illusion. We all believe that goodness overcomes evil. How would it be possible that Christ's life, full of suffering and sacrifice, should end on the cross in agony and pain? If this was all there was to it, then it would be true that there is little difference between the acceptance of a good life or an evil life. In that case what would be life's aim? What would be the point of living? The belief in life hereafter is a faith stronger and greater than all our knowledge. It is a faith that helps and sustains us in all difficulties, it is love as taught by Christ.

That was the sermon as I understood it, and I felt faith entering my consciousness, perhaps I could accept it. I could have a faith such as you never spoke to me about, my dearest parents. This is not a reproach, I would so like to have you here to discuss all this with you. My dear father, I remember well how once you said to me that one day I alone can decide about my faith. It is a hard fight I am fighting on my own, and I thank you for all your past advice and help. I know that in all the world no one has a wiser father than I. You also said that people cling to religion because they are weak and only their belief teaches and helps them to cling to good rather than evil. If all that is true, Father dearest, which of us is strong enough to survive without any faith?

61

I spent Easter holiday 1941 with my sister in Ainsdale. Her English mother and sister went away for a few days, and we acted as housekeepers for her English father, and enjoyed every moment of it. Desmond was a frequent visitor. I felt free after the confines of school. I wrote a long letter to the Allners describing our activities; we could write to Czechoslovakia no longer. But there was always my diary:

We are spending a great deal of time in the company of Mrs Campion's nephew, Desmond, and his friend, Donald. They take us out in the car, far into the country, where we walk and run and eat picnic lunches. Any free time I have, I spend on the bicycle exploring the countryside. I do so wish you could see us, my dearest parents, any fears you may have on our behalf would disappear, for we are truly enjoying life. But I do miss your advice. The other day Věra had a misunderstanding with her English father, Mr Rainford. She was told that she is rather extravagant and was not given six pence to go on a boat (Dorothy received this amount). Věra cried and Mr Rainford consoled her and said she has to learn and fight for what she believes is right. I hugged her and suggested that she gives Mr Rainford a kiss. 'But he did not give me a sixpence,' complained my sister. 'But he consoled you and is kind to you,' said I. So Věra followed my advice, and received a kiss and a sixpence in return and was happy again. I tried to explain to her that at times our pride can be misplaced; I explained how much the Rainfords have done for her and how kind they were. I do hope my parents would have approved with the way I am attempting to bring up their youngest daughter.

Dorothy's four-year-old nephew is with us, I love him. He and I went to church on Sunday, he was so good, and in the middle of the sermon whispered loudly to me: 'Have you got some scent on? I can smell it.'

Věra and I met two Czech soldiers who told us how they escaped from Czechoslovakia. They are so brave. Mrs Campion collected one of them in town and brought him home for us to meet. When she telephoned us we cycled very fast to her house.

The air-raids continue; the poor Londoners are really suffering. So is Liverpool. The other night we too had to hide under the stairs, we could hear the planes and shattering of broken windows. Věra and Dorothy were scared, and in the midst of all this little David whispered: 'Surely my mummy in Bootle is losing her beauty sleep.' Why should such a little child suffer because of mankind's folly? War is so cruel. After the sound of the all-clear we emerged to find all the doors of the house blown in and windows broken. We were so tired, we just removed the glass out of our beds and crawled in to sleep until the morning. Then it was decided that the house was no longer habitable and Mrs Campion came for us to take us to Southport.

So this long episode is being written in Southport. There is never a day free from air-raids. Věra shakes with fear every time the planes fly overhead, so far her recovery from the Ainsdale bombing is slow. One night I stood outside with Desmond, watching the enemy planes, when the bombing started. We both ran immediately to frightened Věra. I laid down next to her and held her close to me. My little sister sighed and said: 'I am so happy.' Warmth flooded my whole being – I felt such joy because she was so happy. Happiness and laughter should be her constant companions – she is young. She is only thirteen years old, but blossoming already, her bosom is larger than mine and she falls in 'love' with every male she meets. I was attempting to tell her what Father explained to me, that she must not be a flirt, but I think I am wasting my breath. I do wish I could consult with my parents about bringing up their daughter. Whenever she is happy I feel so light, when she appears miserable heaviness settles upon me. But it is a happy holiday.

One day Desmond and his mother took us to the beach and we ran and laughed on the sands. Desmond's mother smiled and remarked: 'How happy would your parents be if they could see you now.' I knew this to be true. Yet constant fear for them has become part of me. All the same, during these holidays I have put on weight and my monthly cycle is back to normal. I feel well but sad that in a couple of days Věra and I will have to part again.

May 1941
Another school term. I had to change trains five times on my way to Monmouth. This time I am in a dormitory for only three girls. I am the most senior one and one of the head girls. Another pleasant surprise is that one of my drawings was sent to the War Competition and won second prize. And a friend of Mrs Campion's sent me a watch knowing that I had lost mine. Mrs Allner wrote saying they would love me to live with them when I finish school next year and I could go from their home to a business college. I am so fortunate to have such wonderful friends and am very busy writing letters. Věra too has written asking for advice by return mail – how to deal with a problem. I am glad she turns to me, we squabble often when we are together but we love each other. I managed to get a Czech book for her birthday.

June 1941
The German *Bismarck* has been sunk, Crete is fighting a losing battle, President Roosevelt talked to the whole world and pledged his help to the British and today, 22 June, the Germans have invaded Russia! I know the Russians will not be beaten, but what a war, what a world.

My music teacher from Sandecotes is here on a visit, I am so happy to see her again. I wrote to my ex-schoolmate Catherine who is homesick in her new school. Clothes are being rationed, but the sun is shining. And I think of home whenever I can, but we have so much to learn. I am sitting School Certificate/University Entrance in one week's time (if I pass five subjects including English, my S.C. becomes U.E.). I am glued to books, but was compelled to go cycling with the girls. We covered thirty-six miles, it was terrific.

A fter sitting the examinations, I returned to my diary:

I quite enjoyed the exams. However, in English I chose to do a precis, and found out too late that my English vocabulary is not large enough. Then we had to write about the character of someone we knew well. I wrote about Věra, but after describing her good points I had no time left to mention her bad ones. If I fail this paper I shall have to sit the whole lot again. English literature was good, I quoted by heart from Shakespeare's *Merchant of Venice*.

I liked arithmetic and know for sure that more than half of my answers are correct. The same goes for algebra. I loved the history paper. Among other drawings for the drawing exam, I chose to do a rhododendron from the real flower. I never knew there was so much to see on a real flower. German was good too, though the translation into English was frustrating, it would have been easy had I been translating into Czech. The trouble was that I could not always think of the right English words. But in my German essay I managed to let them know that I am not English.

I received three pounds from Miss Dunn, so I had money to send to the Red Cross. Now that the exams are over, we are busily knitting for the forces, and I have time to read and write and run in the fields and woods with a clear conscience. We also help on the farms with hay-making and give a hand to the gardener who is so busy. I am happy this term. I am busy and get on well with my schoolmates. Ten of them want me to draw into their autograph books, but I am no artist.

I think of my dearest ones, the fear for them is still in my heart but does not now obscure the present I live in – it's hard to explain, but I am sure that you, Mother and Father, would understand. I also know that you wish to see laughter on our faces. I feel you near me, I hear your voices, everything beautiful reminds me of you: when the flowers send out their perfume, when the birds sing to the glory of God, when the breeze plays with my hair – you are there.

I think I would like to be a nurse because I will be able to help in the war effort and learn to do something useful. Mr Herczka thinks my parents would not approve and that I would be constantly in danger. But I am sure that my parents would approve of any profession in which I am content; after all, I know them better than he does, though I am aware that he means well. A secretarial course, which Mr Herczka suggests, would not help the war effort! He is a lovely and kind person, but that does not mean that he understands everything.

As for my sister, I instructed her to send me her letters from the Czech soldiers and her answer to them. Who knows what troubles she would get into otherwise.

The end of term activities are in full swing, I participated in everything, even piano playing. The girls are friendly. After the initial difficulties at the start of the school year, I have found friends and laughter in Uplands, and if I have failed my examinations I shall not mind returning for another year.

If by any chance something should happen to me with all the bombing in Parkstone and Poole, then, Mother and Father, do not be sad. I hope you will read this diary in which I wish to reiterate that I thank you for my life, for my beautiful childhood, happy youth, for all your love and wisdom. You have lived for us and my life belongs to you. My greatest wish is to be able to repay you one day for all that you have done for us.

Do not ever regret sending us to England; much have I learnt here and you know how I yearn to learn. There are happy moments interwoven with sad ones in my life, sorrow as well as laughter walks beside me. Thank you for teaching me about courage, about faith and strength, about love and laughter, with all my heart I thank you for being my parents. May God bless you always.

CHOOSING A CAREER

I left Upland School for a holiday with Bunty and her family. I had to await the result of my examinations and to face a new life away from the shelter of a boarding school. I cherished being in the midst of this family and was grateful that Věra was invited for two weeks. This was August 1941:

We are having such a wonderful time. On the second of this month we received a letter from our father, smuggled out, I am not sure how. He writes that all is well. It is a very short letter. My dearest father, my adored mother, you are my greatest love, for you I live. I hope no letter to us or a smuggled one to you will put you in danger. I would gladly sit in jail here and suffer anything in order to save you having one hair on your head damaged. I cannot describe all the thoughts that went through my head – a mixture of supreme joy and incredible sadness entwined with fear for those at home.

My friends the Allners made sure we had a lovely holiday. I played tennis with Bunty, Věra joined us on walks and picnics, on wet days we played cards, friends came to visit and in spite of daily airraids life seemed good. Věra shared the large double bed I slept in, and before closing my eyes each night I fervently hoped that our parents too had a warm bed to rest in.

The war went on. I helped Mrs Allner to sell 'flags' for bombed-out areas, and felt very grown up when told by a young officer: 'How could I resist such a charming young lady?' That I was no more a child hit me vigorously when Suzanne became engaged, Suzanne with whom I had spent part of my holiday only two years ago:

Are we really growing up so fast? Are we now 'young ladies'? How dreadful, for I shall not be allowed to run with my friends in the street again. Life is going so fast, real childhood is running away, the *real* life beckons. And love – different from a childish love – rests in our hearts. The world of adults confronts me, I am learning, my eyes are being opened, but oh, my father and mother, how I miss your guiding hands, how I wish to see the love in your eyes, feel you near.

Yesterday Mr Churchill and President Roosevelt met in the middle of the ocean to discuss peace plans. They are brave men. The Germans have occupied Smolensk, though the Russians are still fighting there. The Turks have joined Russia and England. For the first time in history Turkey is friendly with the Russians.

We saw a film last night about English raids on German aerodromes. It is dreadful what people do to each other. The second film was *Lady Hamilton*, lover of Nelson. In this film, love won over duty to his wife, and duty to his country took precedence over his love for Lady Hamilton.

The Queen spoke to us, giving us faith, and someone on the radio called Hitler 'Schicklgrüber', his real name.

Miss Dunn sent me five pounds, I was so thrilled because I could give all the money I had to the Red Cross, they need it more than I do. Now I must go to the dentist, my teeth are all right, but need to be examined.

B unty and I had our disagreements. Both in our teens, we were overtaken by tensions neither of us could comprehend, and added to that we decided to eat as little as possible, much to Mrs Allner's worry. When I felt that I might be in Bunty's way and that for some reason she was jealous of me, I suggested to her mother that I return to Ainsdale with Věra, for this was Bunty's home and I did not know how to deal with the situation. 'We would not like that at all,' said Bunty's mother and that settled that. I discussed my problems with the Almighty:

God, I have so many faults and there is no mother and father here to guide me. I worked so hard for School Cert. With little time for anything else. My adorable sister still lies and is so untidy. It is such a responsibility on my shoulders. How shall I bring her up? How can I help her? And how bring up myself? That is even harder. I am not complaining nor am I feeling sorry for myself, I just do not know how to go about it. God, You are the best friend I have, do You hear me?

O f course, Bunty and I made it up, and I did not go away with Věra knowing that to do so would hurt Mrs Allner. But I missed my sister dreadfully. The end of September 1941 arrived:

The Frenchman Laval was shot at. We don't know yet if he was killed. I do not wish anyone any harm, but this war teaches us how to hate. I think that his death might save the lives of hundreds of innocent people. But so far I am unable to pray for anyone's death.

I passed my examinations with credit in English literature, geography, history, and mathematics and distinction in German. And I passed drawing. I received many letters of congratulation, and was so happy and proud, for I kept thinking of my parents and their joy when they heard of my success. Only, when was that to be?

Věra was accepted as a boarder in the one and only Czech school in England. Teachers and professors who had escaped from my country were relieved from the army in order to educate a great number of Czech children, all of them refugees. The school was situated in Hinton Hall, near Whitchurch in Shropshire, and became a home and a secure refuge to all who lived there. It was also a Czech cultural oasis. Věra was among her own people:

Věra sounds so happy. And the Russians are fighting for Leningrad, Odessa and Kiev. The English quietly evacuated 850 inhabitants of Spitsbergen in Norway. I so admire all those fighting for our freedom and I sang heartily hymns of praise during National Thanksgiving Day. So many voices all over England, did you hear us God? Could the war finish without all this killing?

I ceased to be a schoolgirl. I refused to stay another year at school, not wishing to be financially dependant on others, and above all hoping to be allowed to do some work to help the war effort. Miss Dunn would not allow me to join the forces and thought me too young and too fragile to train as a nurse in wartime. My guardian insisted that I had to be trained for something. My only stipulation was that whatever my job was to be, I should be allowed to continue some study and have time for reading. At that stage, I was becoming aware of some discord between Mrs Allner and Miss Dunn, but unaware that I was a pawn in a game. Yet I knew then as fervently as I know now that both had my good at heart in any advice they gave me.

However, it came as a shock when I received a letter from Miss Dunn telling me that I had been accepted for training as a kindergarten nurse in a day nursery in Virginia Water near Windsor, near to where Miss Dunn lived. I had six days to get ready. The thought of living far from my English family was painful, and I was a little fearful of being a part of an institution. I wrote a thank you letter to the Christian Association that freely gave me my schooling and was delighted when their answer came with the comment that my letter was read at their committee meeting.

Bunty too had to make decisions about her future that she found equally difficult, in spite of all the help from her parents. I felt very close to her. The largest cloud on my horizon was Miss Dunn's remark that I would have no time to study further German and French. Watch the dog came with me for our daily walk around the Poole lake and only he witnessed my tears in the dark. I turned to my diary again:

Mother's family. Back row from left to right: Auntie Berta, Grandfather, my uncle, Gustav; front row: my mother, my blind grandmother, my uncle who died young.

The last picture I have of my parents, taken after our departure. They were unable to conceal the sadness in their eyes.

With my mother and sister about a year before our departure.

Tomíček, the young cousin who did not manage to escape to freedom. I do not possess a photo of his older brother, Honza.

My father and mother's cousin Karel in happier times.

Čelákovice u Labe (the river Elbe), where we swam in the summer. We skated on the frozen surface of the river in the winter.

My town of Čelákovice, with my house marked by a cross.

The Prague I frequently visited as a child; Hradčany, the famous castle, can be seen in the background. Karlův Most (Karl's Bridge) is gracing the River Vltava (Moldau).

My class enjoying an outing in Prague, shortly before I left for England. We are standing under Staroměstská Radnice, the famous clock tower. Each hour the twelve Apostles emerge from their hiding place and walk across the face of the clock to the great delight of their audience. I am there, hidden amongst my school friends.

In 1939, before I left for England.

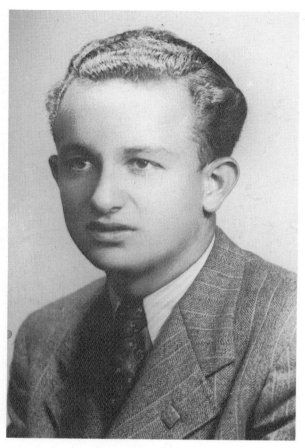

Pepik in 1939. On the back, he wrote, 'To remind you of the beautiful moments of our youth from the one who thinks of you constantly, Pepik.'

With Pepik before our parting on Mstětická Silnice.

With Suzanne in Bournemouth, summer 1939.

Mr Allner (my 'Big Man'), Bunty and Mrs Allner with Watch at their feet.

Miss Dunn with her dog in 1940.

Cedric Allner in 1939.

With Mr and Mrs Rainford, Věra and Dorothy Rainford at our feet, August 1939.

Part of Sandecotes School, my first English school.

Worried about those at home, I was down to six stone (38kg) in the summer of 1940.

Visiting Věra at Easter 1940. My sister was putting on weight; I was losing it.

'The Hendre', the stately home in Monmouthshire, to which Uplands, my second school, was evacuated from Hastings. It was a beautiful place, but, oh, so cold in the winter!

With Věra in 1944.

Date
Datum *2 . V . 1945*

Mark the sentences below thus: ☑   Cocher les phrases ci-dessous ainsi: ☑

Dear *Ina* :   Cher_____ :

☑ I am well and safe.   ☐ Je suis sain et sauf.
☑ Will write as soon as possible.   ☐ J'écrirai dès que possible.
☑ Expect to be home soon.   ☐ J'espère revenir bientôt.
   Do not write.   N'écrivez pas.

Signature *Irma Hammontová*   Signature _____

Merk onderstaande zinnen met een merkteeken; ☑

Beste _____ :

☐ Ik maak het goed en ben veilig.
☐ Zal zoo spoedig mogelijk schrijven.
☐ Verwacht gauw thuis te zijn.
   Schrijf mij niet.

Handteekening _____

A card from Mother, sent from Terezín Fortress.

I loved the sea; not all was sadness.

With 'Granny' Saunders (in bed) and Mrs Harrison, two of my patients.

Roy.

Happy times on my bicycle with Roy.

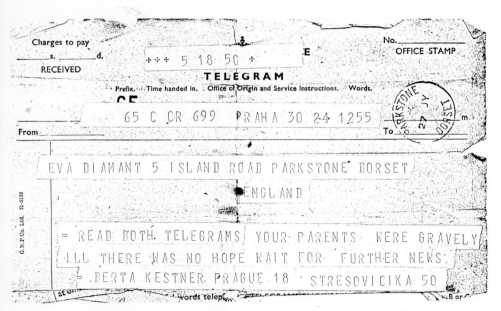

EVA DIAMANT 5 ISLAND ROAD PARKSTONE DORSET
ENGLAND

= READ BOTH TELEGRAMS YOUR PARENTS WERE GRAVELY
ILL THERE WAS NO HOPE WAIT FOR FURTHER NEWS
= BERTA KESTNER PRAGUE 18 STRESOVICIKA 50

The telegram I received telling me of my parents' deaths.

My passport photograph, 1946.

With Pepik in Prague, 1946. I am wearing the same dress Mother had made for me in 1939.

Some of the 200 Czech children whom I took to England in 1946.

My parents' names are on the family plaque, their bones lie in foreign lands, their memory lives in my heart.

Auntie Berta in 1949. Her smiles were always tinged with sadness after the war.

Nicholas Winton when I met him in 1988. I thank him for my life. (Photograph courtesy of *New Zealand News UK.*)

With my husband and children on arriving in New Zealand, 1957.

Life is suddenly hectic. I had to get a doctor's certificate, an insurance card and unemployment card. I also had to report at the police station, the men there are my friends now and wished me well. So did the old shoemaker, he added that we all have to live in hope. And the lady in the sweetshop said she will miss me, but she believes that the war will end soon. Miss Dunn sent me money for the journey, Mr Allner gave me ten shillings and Mrs Allner a new hat.

We had a cable from Cedric from India, the Allners must be worried about him, I do hope nothing will happen to him.

In Czechoslovakia Von Neurath resigned and we have a new protector, Heydrich. On the news they tell us that he is cruel.

It was such a lovely day today, we had a picnic at Swanage and sang hymns in the evening. I feel almost guilty for having enjoyed myself knowing that those at home may be suffering. I shall not forget, I do not forget you my dearest mother and father. Please God, have mercy.

On the 4 October 1941 I found myself at Virginia Water. Miss Dunn met me at the station and took me to the nursery. There I was introduced to the matron and ten 'sisters', and forty-five children. Everyone seemed very friendly and kind. My day started at 6.30am, and with another nurse I was responsible for fifteen children around the age of four. I was told the children were very noisy and very naughty. My heart went out to them, for many were orphans:

I am almost happy here. Yesterday for a while I was alone with seven children, they were so noisy until I suggested I would read them a story. Then they became as quiet as mice. In the afternoon when they were to have a rest, little Michael cried and cried and the other nurse wanted to hit him to stop him making such a noise. I sat on his bed and he told me that he had seen a flash of lightning and was afraid. So I took him in my arms and carried him to the window until he could see the blue sky. He relaxed and went to sleep.

In the evening I had our fifteen children to supervise and put into bed. They are so little, but can make so much noise. When I put the last one into bed, I started singing in Czech. The silence was immediate. I walked singing from bed to bed, and my face was sticky from goodnight kisses. I promised to sing more once I had cleaned the dayroom, and when I returned all my darlings were fast asleep.

We worked until 8pm and then had to do the mending and knitting. The two hours of free time during the day soon went by, as did our half a day off per week. I was exhausted when I collapsed into bed each night. My biggest regret was that I was too tired even to read. I wanted to teach the children, cuddle them, play with them in my way. But obviously there was a protocol that had to be observed. My affection for my charges grew each day, and I felt their love for me. I pondered whether to leave after the first month's trial or whether I should stay. In my short time there, the matron and my co-workers had become my friends. I did not have much time to write in my diary:

I had a short note – how it came I know not – from Auntie Berta saying that she and Mother send their love. My heart sang, but where is Father, why no mention of him? The Germans are nearing Moscow, Heydrich has ordered the execution of twenty of my countrymen, will this war never end? All that I can do is pray and have faith. I must try to do more. How well I see what 'my' children here are missing when I think of my parents. Can a seventeen-year-old girl love them as a mother would?

T hen fate stepped in. Miss Dunn was offered a job elsewhere, and Mrs Allner wrote, saying that the matron of Cornelia Hospital in Poole would accept me as a trainee nurse. My only thought was, 'Now I can do something useful to help to end the war.' After much heart-searching and great debates with the Almighty, I decided to leave my present job:

The matron here said she will find a replacement for me and that, though she will miss me, she too would choose nursing. And Mrs Allner would like me to be near them again . . . I am thinking of the future too. Should I train as a kindergarten nurse and look after other people's children, grow fond of them and then have to part from them again? How many times would my heart get broken? As a nurse I would be of more use to England and after the war at home.

Miss Dunn sent me such a nice letter. About my decision she wrote, 'Needless to say I am thinking much about you and do want you to do what is for the best. I certainly do not want to stand in your way of starting hospital training if you feel that is what you want to do. As you know, my reason for turning you from it at first was that I was just afraid you would find it too hard, at any rate until you were a little older. However, I am quite ready to agree that I was probably wrong and that it may turn out to be no harder than what you are doing now.

There is one point that may influence you . . . I do not think I shall be in this neighbourhood for long. I shall be back at a school . . . I shall fall in with whatever you decide, for I know that you will have tried honestly to do what is best – and after all, honesty, not only to other people, but to ourselves also, is one of the most important things in the world.

Now go ahead, make your own decision and you will have my blessing upon it. I shall be thinking of you on Friday – it is to be my great day too,

70

so just give me a thought of good wishes. Always yours affectionately Margaret Dunn.'

I am so happy for Miss Dunn that she is able to return to teaching again. As for me, I shall miss the children and this place. Here I have made friends among the people I work with as well as people outside the institution. In Poole I would be near my English family. Anyhow, nursing in a hospital would be helping the war effort and that is what I need to do to help those at home.

T hus the die was cast.
During my last month in Virginia Water, one of my free days was spent with Mr Herczka, whom I had not met for a long time. He never received my letter informing him of my planned visit. His delight when he saw me compensated for the struggle I had to find his flat. When I realized that his meal consisted of dry bread and a cup of cocoa, I decided to send him any rations I might have. I eventually did this, feeling that this was the least I could do for him.

We talked about my parents, my Auntie Berta, whose friend he was, and his life. He was a German Jew, he never wanted to return to Germany, and he knew that the Czechs would not want to accept German-speaking people:

Mr Herczka said to me, 'After the war I might as well hang myself.' This was the first time I heard of his dilemma. I answered, 'That is the last thing you need to do, for that there is plenty of time.'

I don't believe that my countrymen would reject people like him. I feel so sorry for him and feel such affection for him. I see in him a Jew, a businessman with a kind heart who deprives himself in order to give to others. I see in him a person whom the Germans hate for his wisdom. Mr Herczka told me that I am a clever and pretty girl, that I should marry in England and make my home here. I am too young to marry, and though I know well that life in England would be easier, Czechoslovakia is my home. Apart from that, I could never marry except for love. I have not lost all my ideals!

Mr Herczka does not object to my being a nurse, as long as I have nothing to do with infectious diseases. I don't think about that, but I know that I can look after others with a smile on my face and give them help and courage.

I missed the last bus on my way home and had to walk from the station. It was pitch dark and misty, yet I could see some stars. I thought of those at home and of the little children still under my care. I feel so sorry for them. One two-year-old girl misses her mother so much; because I cuddle her she follows me everywhere, I am told not spoil her. Can loving spoil? Some of the children are here because their mothers are working. Somehow it seems wrong, little children need a mother, no matter how

71

poor. If I stayed here I would soon be accused of hugging them too much. I try to buy things for those who don't seem to have anyone.

A few days later a letter arrived from my sister. Now nearly fourteen years old, Věra wrote that she so much missed our mother – and I sensed that something was amiss. I had enough knowledge of her not to ask what was wrong, but replied at once and mentioned that I too missed our parents dreadfully. In the next letter Věra confessed her dilemma, she was in love, but would Mother be angry that she had a boyfriend? She reminded me that I had a boyfriend at home and was not forbidden the relationship. The truth was that I refused to be forbidden! I knew that to forbid Věra a friendship with a boy would be futile. I could base my advice only on that which I had received:

'It has to be only a friendship, for a real love you have to wait till you are eighteen years old – as Father asked of me. And if this at times seems too difficult, think of our parents.'

How I understand my 'little' sister. I feel again her age, and remember running in the woods and meadows with Pepik. Please God, look after my sister. She is thirsty for her mother's love, don't let her throw away her childhood and embrace a love that could give her pain and sorrow. For that she has plenty of time.

I did not tell Věra that I read in the newspapers that inhabitants of our home town had all radios confiscated because they were found listening to the English broadcast. I so fear for them all, I feel so helpless. My life used to be a fairytale and now I have to face the hard reality alone. I do not speak of my fears to those around me. All I can do is pray to the God of all.

At the end of October 1941, a month before I was to leave the kindergarten, I received my first salary for the month: one pound, nineteen shillings and nine pence:

I feel rich. Now I can send a donation to the Red Cross. The rest I have to save for my journey to Poole.

By chance I met three Czech airmen in Windsor, we went to a coffee house. I was delighted to speak Czech again. They joked and teased me, we laughed together but I felt there was also fear and pain underneath their rough exteriors. I did not know how to tell them that I am so grateful to them for fighting for our freedom.

I spent a day in London with Miss Dunn, visiting famous places. I was thankful for this day and time to talk to her. Miss Dunn still thought I was too young for nursing and might not be able to 'stick' it.

Back at the hospital the children had colds and influenza, and we were very busy. I felt my need to show them my deep love for them, and I felt their need to receive it. I prayed that those who had parents would return to them and that the orphans should find a happy home. Many a prospective adoptive parent came and left empty-handed. Some of them seemed to be looking for beauty of the face, a child to show off rather than a child to love.

November arrived and with it my father's birthday:

11.11.1941
Can you feel my kisses, Father dearest? Do you know of my thoughts, my wishes for you? May God protect you always, please be strong, be happy, don't worry about us. I send my love to you and Mother by the moon and the stars. I shall try never to let you down so that you can always be proud of me. I do wish I were a better person, though I know no one can be perfect. But I would like to be what *you* want me to be . . .

13.11.1941
Today is your birthday, my dear granny. You used to think me so naughty, and you loved us so much. I think of your stories, your wonderful cooking, your great courage. To you I send all the best wishes in the world. I see you on our last day in Prague, how you waved goodbye to us, shall we meet again? I remember the past but have to live in the present.

With the girls here I walk and cycle during our free time, and last Sunday we went to the Congregational church. I liked the sermon. The minister pointed out that how we pray and how we think has a great influence on what kind of people we become. What do you believe, Father? You, Mother, you always had a great faith. The minister finished with something funny, he said: 'Most people go to church only three times: when they are baptized, when they marry and when they die. In the first and last situation they are unconscious and in the second nearly so.'

The end of November arrived, and I parted with my friends and 'my' children crying as much as they did. And thus I returned to the Allners. As I was a 'friendly alien' I had to receive permission from the Home Office to work in the hospital. This arrived ten days later.

WITH TEA LIKE THIS
YOU WILL NEVER CURE
THE ENGLISH

On 7 December 1941 Pearl Harbour was bombed, America entered the war and I started my nursing training at Cornelia Hospital. My predominant thought, recorded in my diary, was, 'With America on our side, surely this senseless killing will soon cease.' We worked from 7.30am, after breakfast, till 8.30pm, when we went for supper. During the day, the two hours off duty included lectures. I had a little room of my own, but was not permitted to open the windows because of black-out. Loving fresh air, I found this a hardship. Working on a children's ward – seeing children get better and knowing that I helped a little – was a compensation. I felt especially pleased when a little boy whispered, 'I do like you.' But I was not a born nurse and was very ashamed when I fainted a couple of times on seeing wounds.

My first hospital Christmas was an unforgettable experience. The staff went out of their way to make it a happy day for the patients; many presents were given and received. Even I was laden with gifts, and felt part of a whole. When in the evening I walked with another nurse to the Allners to wish them a Happy Christmas, to give them my gifts and receive theirs, I felt my parents were close and knew that they would be happy for me. And they would have been happy for Věra, for my sister wrote that she was overjoyed in her Czech school.

On New Year's Eve I danced and danced at the hospital party. And at midnight, with New Year's Day, came my eighteenth birthday. More than my own, I felt my parents' pain at not being able to celebrate this day with me. I thought of them and remembered Pepik, wondering if the affection we felt for each other as children would grow into something deeper. To my parents I could send only twenty-five words via the Red Cross, not knowing whether they would reach their destination. 'Do they know I am a nurse? Would they approve?' I asked whilst donning my uniform.

Cornelia Hospital in Poole housed over 200 patients in an old building, which was built in 1906 on a site donated by Lord and Lady Wimborne. Lady Cornelia, who gave Poole its first hospital in 1889, officially opened it in May 1907. The wards were long, with seventeen to twenty beds on each side. With the men and children, the medical and surgical cases shared the same wards. The women were privileged, they had separate medical, surgical and maternity departments. Cornelia was a fantastic training school for nurses, and if one had to be sick this was the place to go to.

Our four-year training included participation in all the departments. Thus we worked not only on all the wards but also in the theatre, out-patients and X-ray departments and assisted the psychiatrists with their patients who were treated as out-patients.

Visitors were permitted only on Sundays and Wednesdays for two-and-a-half hours. The same rule also applied to the children. It was believed that this was kinder to them and would help them settle more quickly. As a result, we often acted as surrogate parents to the long-staying youngsters.

Matron Lambert was in charge of the hospital, and her responsibility encompassed everything and everyone under its roof. This included the care of all the patients, and the employment and behaviour of the nursing and domestic staff. It was the matron who counted the linen and ascertained that there was enough food. Small wonder I never saw her walk! Always in a hurry, she kept her finger firmly placed on the pulse of all that she surveyed.

I made friends at work, went for long walks by the sea, played tennis till daylight faded, visited the Allners whenever possible and loved the sick children in my care. There was so much to learn, so much to see, so much to know about illnesses and how to help the sick return to health. I rejoiced when 'my' children were well enough to go home and cried my heart out over those whom we could help no more:

11.1.1942

I dream of my home at night and am so busy during the day. One little boy went home today, he said he would not go home without me! Of course he went. For little Michael I do everything myself, it is such a wonderful feeling to see the children on their way to recovery. After a month here I am already allowed to do some dressings, and soon will be the second senior. I want to know everything and learn as much as I can and do not mind working overtime, though we do not get any overtime pay. With my first salary I bought a present for Věra and for Mr Herczka, the rest I am saving to go towards a bicycle.

This contrariness in human beings puzzles my silly brain. There is so much killing and hatred in the world: and so much love and pity. Here I see the inventions that save life, and out there bombs, also invented by men, kill thousands. Have our heads run away with our hearts?

I still cry now and then when I think of home, but my faith that God will spare them is strong. I have forgotten to write down that from my salary I also sent ten shillings to the Red Cross. We receive two pounds, six shillings and eight pence a month. But I don't need anything for myself.

I do so love you, my dearest parents. How can I ever reciprocate your great and unselfish love? You thought only of us, never of yourselves. From a young country lad who stole pears from trees, grew my dearest father, and through determination and hard work he built a thriving business. And a beautiful little girl, whose youth was spent looking after her blind mother and little brother, became our hard-working mother. You are so good and kind, I am not worthy of you. Just keep your fingers crossed that at least you do not need to be ashamed of me.

I have to write to Věra who is asking for advice about how to explain something to Mrs Campion without hurting her feelings. Mrs Allner seems worried about me, tells me I work too hard, look tired and thin and don't get enough sleep. When I am tired, the fear for those at home seems to be harder to deal with.

I am saving for my holidays, so I walked the four miles to the dentist to save on bus fares. His bill will be big enough!

I n January we received, via the Red Cross, twenty-five words written in German from our mother:

Mother says they are all right. But are they? I feel my mother's love, I know that my parents' hearts beat only for us. I feel I am nothing without them, it is their picture that I carry in my soul that gives me strength to go on living. Will I ever be able to make up to them for all that they have done for us? I miss them so. Everyone has weak moments. It is the past that gives us courage in the present to fight for a better future. To cry now and then and long for home is not a sign of weakness. It is a sign of love and to love is not shameful.

Just now I feel I am not a born nurse. I like my patients and am so glad I am able to help them, but I wish I had more time for books other than nursing ones. Often I am too tired to read. When the air-raids come we have to move all the beds into the corridors, and if they come at night most of us prefer to help on the wards rather than sit in the shelters.

I don't mind the work, but I long for fresh air. Being indoors all day and having to sleep with my window shut is a real punishment. I must stop thinking about myself and think of the poor parents of the three-month-old little girl who died in our ward. I could have cried with them. This was my first 'death', will I ever become used to seeing people die? Just now, my heart feels tight and I cannot eat. But I must persevere; others work happily and so will I. Once my tasks involve more nursing and some responsibility rather than washing and cleaning, then I'll surely begin to feel more like a nurse. I will get used to seeing blood and smelly wounds.

Today I held the hands of little Pamela, who had an abdominal dressing changed after peritonitis. When all was finished I fainted and pulled her out of bed on top of me. Pamela thought it funny, but I was so ashamed and ten minutes later was back at work. I seem to be losing my memory. If this war does not finish soon I'll not be able to guarantee my sanity.

15.1.1942
I am sending a note to my mother via the Red Cross, hoping that she will

receive it for her birthday in March. At times I am so filled with fear for her, I am not sure that the signature on her last message was not falsified. My heart aches, please, God, have mercy, bless and do not desert my dearest parents.

31.1.1942

I try so hard to get on top of things, but my head aches, my eyes are sore and I am incredibly tired. I lack the strength to carry out my duties, though I love the children who also seem to be fond of me. Was Miss Dunn right? Is nursing too hard for me? I must not give in. It is not only the work but the fear for those at home that adds to my feeling of weakness and lack of energy.

Mid-March 1942

I had such a nice letter from my sister. Věra writes that I am so good to her and am a real parent to her and that she knows I too miss my parents. Věra says she is happy in her Czech school surrounded by people who also have no parents in England. Apparently she enquired if I could also join her. She was told that I would be welcomed with open arms because my Czech is good and I am a good student, and after a year or so there I could go to university here or at home. This would be one dream come true, to be with Věra, among my own countrymen, and be able to study. Věra says this way I could also be of help to England and later to my country. With all my being I wish to join Věra; yet, I am doing something very necessary and useful here, matron would be anything but pleased if I left. Mrs Allner feels I should not be spending taxpayers' money on being educated when at the age of eighteen I can earn my own living. Mr Allner asks, 'Are you happy in the hospital, Little Girl?' I have not got the heart to say to him, 'Not just now,' and so give an evasive reply.

I hope to spend my forthcoming holiday with Věra and talk things over. I feel I cannot let Mrs Allner down, though Miss Dunn wrote and said I have her blessing on whatever I choose to do. What I choose may not be what I so much wish for. Where does duty lie, is it ever clear? Věra keeps writing, begging me to come. She says I had done so much for her and she would like to do this for me, for she knows I would be happier in her school. How right she is.

I have friends here, we walk, we talk, yet I do not seem able to talk of the pain in my heart nor of my problems, I prefer to listen to theirs. Why should I burden them with mine?

W hen Bunny, a friend with whom I went for long walks and played tennis, said that my hair looked like gold in the sunshine, I felt content, especially as the next day there was a hospital dance. When we were at home, about a year before we left for England, mother had long pink dresses made for Věra and me, as we were to be bridesmaids for a cousin. I wore this dress for every dance during the war; I could not afford any other. It was a very pretty garment, its only drawback being the dozens of little buttons marching from the back of my neck to under my waist. I could neither dress nor undress on my own! I danced and danced, but refused to make a date or to be taken back after the dance, fearing that I might lose my heart to an Englishman and thus jeopardize my return home.

A new nurse joined our staff, and with Ann Carter, my new friend, I also went for long walks, our favourite pastime, often climbing in through windows at night as the doors were locked by 10pm.

In April 1942 another short message reached us from mother, asking us why we did not write. We realized that our letters had not been reaching our parents. There was nothing we could do. Both Věra and I prayed to God to give them courage and protect them from all evil. Later I read in the papers that any letters sent to Czechoslovakia, even through the internationally recognized channels, could cause the death of an entire family. Apparently, no matter how innocent the content of such letters, the recipients had on many occasions been charged by the German authorities with espionage. Czechs in England were warned by the Czech Government not to write home. We could not risk our parents' lives, so letters home had to stop.

At work we were more than busy. Hardly a night passed without German bombers flying over our heads, and our hospital was full of innocent victims. 'Can we not solve our differences in a peaceful fashion?' I asked my diary. I cried when two young boys died in our ward as a result of the bombing. Unfortunately, many more injured were to pass through my hands.

In spite of the tragedies, there was also much joy confessed to my diary:

A little homesick girl wanted to go home. I told her she would be going tomorrow. So all day today she cried, 'Tomorrow is today.' Little Rodney keeps hugging me, and Diana and Peter tell me that they belong only to me. I nursed little Mary in my arms to send her to sleep, her head resting on my shoulders. Only when I put her down on her bed, did I remember that her head was full of nits. I wonder how many I inherited! I feel again this great warmth when surrounded by 'my' children's love and embrace them with my own. All this fighting cannot kill loving. I only wish that the tiredness would leave me.

In May 1942 I became a patient myself with jaundice. I almost collapsed on my feet before they carried me to bed. I felt sick and was feverish, food tasted awful and my body ached. However I was aware of little heads peeping through the door and a profusion of flowers in my room, which was adjacent to the children's ward. The staff also came to visit me, and my friends the Allners transferred me to their home to recuperate as soon as the doctor allowed. I was sick for four weeks and emerged from the ordeal as a skeleton, in spite of all the loving care I had received. The Germans systematically bombed Poole. So that we could get some sleep, the matron altered her rule and permitted us to stay in bed during the raids. Our shelters were empty and we took it in turns to help on the wards. On 10 June I heard on the radio that Lidice in Czechoslovakia was wiped out as a retribution for Heydrich's assassination in May: our 'Protector' was killed by persons unknown. 1200 people died in Lidice and 350 more were executed for a variety of reasons. It was believed that the total number of deaths was much higher, as many executions were not reported.

A week later, I was back at work in the children's ward:

When I told matron that I still ache and have a piercing pain in my side, she replied that at work I'll not have time to think about myself! How right she was. There is little Derek who needs a skin-graft on his leg damaged by falling debris during bombing; and little Irene who lost her sight in both eyes for a few days after her granny dropped her when the bombs damaged their house; and there is two-year-old Rodney who keeps asking me to cuddle him. I love them all, even five-year-old Michael who is very naughty and even spits at us. No wonder, poor boy, he seems to have no one who cares for him.

On 22 June 1942, Tobruk fell into German hands. Seventy-three more Czechs were executed because of Heydrich's death. Cedric was in India having survived the fighting in Burma. I shared the relief felt by 'my' family. The Germans were less than ten miles from Egypt's frontiers. The English sent 1000 planes to bomb Bremen and lost over fifty-two of them. We wondered what the repercussions would be.

29.6.1942

I remember three years ago when we left home. I think of all those at home, bring their faces to my memory and pray for their survival. When will all this cruelty end? In her letter Věra says that she does not know what she would do without me, that I do make up to her for the absence of Mother and Father, but I am not her mother and father. How well I understand, no one can take the place of our dear parents. She misses them and so do I, so very much. I try so hard to do what I think they would want of me, but at times it is hard to be good and kind. I must try to be better than I am, less selfish. How I wish I could talk to you, Father. Yesterday in his sermon, the vicar said that it is not always the person who reaches all his worldly goals who is happy. A good person, even if defeated, can reach great happiness.

My faith is so small and perhaps not even the right kind of faith, but I feel I would be really lost without my faith in God. He gives me courage and forgives my follies. I know so little, there is so much to learn, so much to discuss with you, Father dearest. May God bless you and Mother.

One more thing. Peter's mother brought some chocolates, which she shared among the children, and I also received a small piece. Giving sweets to the children is forbidden, but I felt a little would do them no harm; they enjoyed it and so did I. This moment reminded me of the time when I was sick with scarlet fever in a Prague hospital, we too enjoyed sweet things! Did I do wrong, Father? Should I have forbidden the kind lady her generosity? I hope you would not reprimand me for enjoying with her the glee on the children's faces.

I spent my holiday in July 1942 with my sister at Hinton Hall, where her Czech school found its haven. During the school holidays, the crumbling stately home was turned into a camp, for many of the children had nowhere else to go. Nor did the teachers have any other home. So I joined Věra's Czech family. My diary is full of happy impressions:

I don't know how to describe this wonderful feeling of being with my darling sister. Věra is only two centimetres shorter than me, but she is bigger and has really blossomed out. I hear Czech everywhere and eat Czech food. I've been only a few days here, but this feeling of belonging is incredibly strong. I feel free, am amongst my own, who understand the unspoken pain. I run in the woods and the fields, go to the friendly village and am surrounded by Czech books that I read till the early hours of the morning. Again I am called Eva Diamantová, the name that the English find so hard to pronounce. Everywhere else I am the foreigner, the refugee, but not here. And the teachers literally beg me to stay because I love learning and speak perfect Czech. Some of the pupils come from Sudetenland and their first language is German. Every fibre in my body longs to stay, to study again in this environment, amongst my own people and with Věra. I could train as a doctor in England if the war goes on, if it finishes in time then in Czechoslovakia. Věra too begs me to stay, and within my breast another battle is taking place. I remember Mrs Allner's words that I should earn my living instead of depending on the taxpayer. I know that I am helping to finish this war by nursing. When I return I shall be in the men's ward and among my patients will be those injured in battle. I have learnt a great deal and know that I am a good nurse now. Here I am being told that after the war my country will need well-educated young people because those at home are deprived of proper education.

Mother and Father, another crossroad. What would you wish me to do? Follow my heart and stay, or do my duty as I see it and carry on nursing? I cannot hear your voices so I have to make my choice alone.

A few days later, I decided I could not shirk my duty. Having started nursing I felt I had to continue. Half of me agreed with my decision, the other half cried bitter tears. I felt I could have made no other choice. I thought of those suffering in the hospital, of the students around me who also had no news of their loved ones, and I debated: 'Why is it that when one feels one's own pain one forgets other people's pain? It should be quite the reverse. After all, when one shares the pain of others, one forgets one's own sorrow.' My decision to continue nursing was greatly influenced by Mrs Allner's reply to my letter in which I mentioned my desire to study at the Czech boarding school:

My dearest Eva,
Your letter yesterday was a great surprise and I have been thinking about it ever since . . . I was surprised that you could think of giving up the hospital after having signed on. When you knew about the Czech school before signing on, you decided to stay at the hospital, and now it seems to me you have given your word and can only break it if you were able to go home, as that was the condition made before you went there. Another consideration is that you are almost due to register for war work, and if going back to school exempts you I don't think it ought. If you stay at the school, who pays for you and do they find you a job afterwards? Whoever pays, I think a much better use could be made of the money than sending back to school a girl of your age who is perfectly capable of earning her own living and being useful in the world. After all, we are not put here for our own enjoyment, but to do the greatest possible good to the greatest number of people, or in some cases to give up our lives to perhaps just one person. No one can make up your mind for you unless you are extremely weak willed, and if you decide to give up your obligations, it is *you* doing it and you must not say you could not help it.

You asked me to say just what I think, and I have. I am not angry with you or 'blowing you up', and I want always to be your English mother and this your English home, and I feel very sorry that you are faced with this great temptation. I should certainly not have been so pleased for you to have this holiday had I known. I don't think I will say any more today, but will wait for your next letter, but if you are writing to Miss Dunn or matron please tell them I think you should stay in the hospital.

With much love, dear child, and may God guide you to do what is right. Your English mother who finds her Czech daughter a little difficult sometimes!

P.S. Read Psalm 15.
Don't forget you have been given a year's holiday for much less than a year's work.

A fter receiving my letter stating that I would continue nursing, I received a swift reply. Here are parts of that letter:

My dearest Eva,
I am sure you have done the right thing and I am proud of you. I know it was not easy and I hate to think of you being disappointed.
... We have had two letters from Cedric written in May, when he was still in the wilds of India unable to send a cable or buy even a pocket handkerchief or have a meal except out of a tin! He told us about the retreat from Burma, the Japs tried to stop them crossing the river Chinguin and they had to destroy everything they could not carry and march all night through the jungle and cross the river higher up. There they found some motor transport that had got across earlier, and he said he was lucky as he had to walk only forty miles. He does not say how many of them escaped, but I gather he was with a small party ...
We shall all be very pleased to see you.
    With much love to you and Věra. Yours affectionately O. Allner

I am back at the hospital. It was so obvious to me that all the teachers wished I would come back at the beginning of the school year, not only because I am a good student but also because they seem fond of me. I shall always miss the cultural Czech oasis in England. On my way back I met Hanka in London; she is a friend from the Czech school. We talked and talked before my second train for Bournemouth arrived – I missed the first on purpose.
    At present I am working on the women's medical ward and at times am left in charge. It takes all my ingenuity to deal with three doctors arriving at the same time, as well as a dying patient and another one who should be in a maternity ward as she went into labour in my ward. I moved her just in time before the baby arrived. This is wartime, we are short of staff, short of beds, short of everything except goodwill, and life goes on.
    Yesterday I wrote to my sister, I owed her three letters. Hopefully I have made up for it by sending twelve pages. I wrote about faith that gives us courage, about love for our fellow men, love for our parents, even about love between men and women. I tried to explain about love that is the basis of miracles, without which one cannot live. I hope I explained what I meant and that my letter helps my sister.
    Girls of my age are married, some of them, anyhow. I still feel a child. Yet I know that my aim is not to be a liberated woman. I hope for a family of my own, a husband to love and children to bring up. That is for the future. In the present I feel myself blossoming when surrounded by friends, when surrounded by love. That is why I was happy in the Czech school. In love we are conceived, only love gives meaning to life. I am only just beginning to have an inkling of what life is all about. I am trying to understand, in my head so many ideals are taking shape, life seems too

short to grasp everything and to put into practice some of it.

August 1942
A few days ago I received letters from the teachers at the Czech school and from Věra, asking me to reconsider and to join them. Instead of sticking to my resolution to carry on nursing, thoughts keep invading my head and temptation creeps in. My thoughts run like this:

I would love to learn more, understand more, sharpen my brain. As an educated person I could be of great help to my nation after the war and to England if the war goes on. And I would spend the next year with Věra in a Czech surrounding.

But, I am already doing something useful and helpful in this fight for freedom. I am helping England, which has given me so much. I am beginning to like nursing, have friends here, am fond of my patients, feel needed and am earning my own money. I think I would feel guilty if I left now, I seem to have a remarkable conscience that would not allow me to study in peace. How I wish I could talk this over with my parents. When I look at the sick in my care I *know* that I want to help them and that I know how to help them and can do so now. If I study only, become an intellectual, I shall most probably understand, or think that I understand, the past, history, etc., etc., but I may not know how to 'lay my hand to a plough'. So many people lead good lives without high education. I can always nurse at home after the war, or I could study then, should the opportunity present itself. Even Mr Herczka now joins Mrs Allner in telling me to stay. He writes, 'Only the rich can afford to study. As a nurse you will be able to work anywhere in the world.'

For me the pointers seem to go in both directions. So, God, I'll leave it to You to decide, or rather, to help me to choose. If You exist, and I believe that You do exist, please help me to make a decision that I will never regret.

I stayed.
In August 1942, Churchill visited Stalin in Moscow, and Brazil joined the fight. The Duke of Kent was killed in a plane crash together with sixteen others, and no one knew whether or not it was an accident. The Germans were approaching Stalingrad.

3.9.1942
I am busy on the women's surgical ward. Some of the staff went to a church service, but I had to stay on duty. That has not prevented me from sending a silent prayer to the Almighty: 'Please God, make us worthy of victory.'

Already I have been given a great deal of responsibility at work. We are very busy and the air-raids continue, at times averaging six per day and night. Mrs Allner is again complaining that I look pale and tired and that I should spend my free time (what there is of it) resting. But I long for fresh air. I think of home, of the dear ones there, and hope for the end of this foolish war. At times I feel that I live more in the future than the present – a state of affairs that should not go on. I have to think of all the nice things around me. The smiles of patients, that one of them is darning my stockings, the chocolates they give us as a sign of appreciation . . .

We are asking for one day off per week instead of a half day only, I do hope our request will be granted. Before this week is out I am going on night duty. What will that be like?

End of October
I had no time to write whilst working on night duty, for four weeks we kept going without any nights off. Then I slept at the Allners.

I'll try and tell you, my diary, of some of the happenings of the last few weeks. My first duties at night were on the children's ward. Most of the time I was there alone, doing the dressings, giving injections, feeding the children their breakfast. I hardly had time to sit down during the eleven hours, and time went very quickly. We have two new housemen, both very kind and very friendly and quite young. I have learnt to trust myself and get on with my tasks; I can see you smiling, my dearest Mother and Father, I do hope that you will not be disappointed in me.

After three weeks with my twenty-nine children I was moved to the maternity ward. It scared me at first – what a lot of pain you mothers go through so that a child can be born. You love the child, bring it up and send it into the world. I think of you, my very own mother, of all your love and care. May the day come when I will be allowed to tell you how much I value what you are, how grateful I am that *you* are my mother. I used to be so naughty and often rude, have you forgotten this, have you forgiven me? You are such a fighter. On the surface your life seemed ordinary, and yet I see now how you fought the everyday fights, how you enveloped those around you with your love. You loved your parents and helped your blind mother so much with not only words but deeds. You devoted your life to your husband, I know that you would gladly lay down your life for him. You adored your little brother, whom you alone brought up; his death at the age of twenty-one left you devastated. And you had endless love for us, the greatest love, which forced you to give us up regardless of your breaking heart. All your life you have bestowed love on others, and this love has cost you so many tears, so much pain. I did not understand in the past, I do understand now and am helpless, for there is no way to calm your fears, ease whatever burden you are asked to carry. May God bless you and Father. Sleep well.

Whenever I feel tired I think more of home, worry more about those who are undoubtedly suffering there. Only by working hard here can I help. But I fall asleep anywhere, over my lecture books, when sorting out the linen, and now I have slept for twenty-four hours after the four weeks on night duty. I am enjoying my free time; I run in the park with Watch, go for walks and to the cinema with my friends, and I breathe fresh air. I even have time to read books that aren't for study. I read Shakespeare and Bernard Shaw, the latter is full of sarcasm, but I like his books. I feel almost happy and full of hope.

I am getting used to the maternity ward. One woman was angry because she wanted a girl but produced a boy, maybe that is why she made more noise than most. When she was given an injection she declared; 'and with all this pain they stick a pin into me'. The English have a funny sense of humour. When I dished out somewhat weak tea for my patients, our Sister poured it down the sink and pronounced, 'With tea like this you will never cure the English.'

We still have many air-raids and many injured – many dying. In pain we are born, in pain we die and much pain we suffer through life. I never thought that at the age of eighteen years I would know so much and at the same time learn that I really know so very little.

I have seen my first caesarean section performed, the operation where a baby comes into this world through a cut in the abdomen. It is so quick, so fantastic. A wound, and before you know where you are, there is a little crying infant. It is a real miracle.

I continued on night duty and worked in the men's ward. It was a long ward, with seventeen patients on each side and six on a balcony. I was delighted to be there:

The men don't make half as much noise as the women. Here we have a sixty-one-year-old grandfather with a clot on his brain, he is rebellious, poor man, and does not know what he is doing. And a much younger man is lying in plaster of Paris with a broken spine and never complains. We nurse fathers without legs and old gentlemen who had super pubic operations. We look after diabetics, after soldiers and airmen who are either sick or hurt in battle. I love them all, except a lieutenant who thinks he deserves special treatment because of his rank. We too shall get used to each other.

I was called four times from my evening meal at midnight, which we cook ourselves and eat on the ward. My stomach must be pretty good!

Among our patients is a reverend, who on his way to visit the sick fell off his bicycle and fractured his leg. He is such a nice, white-haired fifty-one-year-old gentleman. On the balcony a man is dying from tuberculosis and broncho-pneumonia. His breathing is dreadful, rattling, he sweats and is taking so long to die, poor man. The men near him feel helpless, we can do little to help. I give him water, turn him, wash him, hold his hand and feel that I am slightly easing his departure from this world.

Now I had better write to my dear sister. I have a horrid cold.

85

EVEN THOUGH A PERSON IS NINETEEN YEARS OLD ...

B efore the end of 1942, we received a very short letter, just a few words, from our mother. This message was sent to Mr Herczka via Switzerland:

Mother calls me her good independent girl and says she is proud of me. So they know I am nursing, they must have had some of our earlier letters. What a terrific present for Christmas and for my birthday. Truly, I could not ask for more. Yet I fear for them.

T hat page of my diary was smothered by tears. The new year arrived:

The days are so impatient to get here, it is 1943. I wonder what this year holds in store for us.

At the hospital we had a couple of dances before Christmas Day. I was in great demand, but refused to make a date with anyone. Maybe one day I shall say 'yes'. Besides, just now I need my free time for sleep. One of my old patients calls me his 'sunshine' and another one his 'little lady'. The latter gave us each five shillings before going home to die, his cancer is incurable. His wife asked me to visit them, I'll need much courage to do so. Horace wrote me a verse:

I would like to say
a lot to you
but as the space
is only small
you will have
to find it all
in 'thank you'
that is all!

And Ivan Green, the airman, also wrote me a verse and entitled it:

TO THE SWEETEST OF THEM ALL
The days of waiting have gone past
For Sunday next I go at last.
Before I go, let me convey –
My thanks to you in every way.
Your carefree smile and voice so sweet,
Have helped to put me on my feet.
And deep inside me – further more
I'll keep your memory – ever more.
   To nurse Diamant with my sincere thanks.

I was thrilled with them both.

Nowadays when I walk in Poole I am no longer a stranger, so many of the people I meet are ex-patients. Just before Christmas we had eight new patients, hurt during bombing. Among them was a fourteen-year-old boy who succumbed to his wounds the next day. I talked with a patient called Roy and said how dreadful this endless bombing was. Roy replied that we do the same to the Germans. What a consolation! Mankind has lost all its senses. Life is so short and yet we treat each other in this way, are full of hatred and malice instead of understanding and tolerance in spite of our differences.

After working for four weeks on night duty with no nights off I was given two free nights to spend with Věra. My sister was here for two weeks. I can hardly describe my joy at seeing her; we talked about our home, about our parents, and I heard about her school and all her doings. And we could talk in Czech. Věra looks much more grown up and seems to be more serious, the laughter does not come so readily. Mother and Father, how can I possibly take your place, how can I be a good parent to your second daughter? We are almost equal now, Věra is a child no more.

I was so sad when my sister left, I miss her so. She admired my uniform, but does not know what kind of work we have to do.

The days are not long enough, we have little time for sleep, for we also like to go for walks, to the pictures, etc. 'We' means the nurses I work with who are called Gempton, Tricia and Maskell. Here we call each other by our surnames. No one can pronounce 'Diamantová' so I am called Di.

Something else I must add to this long chapter: I have met a Mrs Frank who is Czech. She said to me, 'You are only a babe and already are doing such important and heavy work.' I don't know about that, but I am so glad to have met her. More good news – I was called in on the maternity ward where a Mrs Somogyi gave birth to a son. She is a Moravian married to a Slovak.

I am trying to read a great deal and read good books. One day I would so like to write a book myself. I feel I have so many thoughts and ideals in my head that I should defend against all critics. I have this subconscious feeling that maybe, one day, I shall do something good in this world.

I n January 1943, Churchill and Roosevelt met secretly, and Churchill spoke of 'the end of the beginning'. With the battle of Stalingrad in February 1943, the tide of war had changed. Hitler's dream of world domination had ended, he was now fighting only to save his neck.

I have been too busy when on duty and too sleepy when off to write anything. After four weeks of working with no nights off I now have four free days and nights and am with my friends the Allners. When I arrived I retired to sleep for eighteen hours.

Last month I have worked not only in the men's ward but also on the children's ward. Poole has had much bombing; one night fifteen injured were brought in. My concern was for the children, but I need not have worried. The older ones were pacifying the younger ones, and I found only one boy hiding under the bed! My three-year-old Jimmy who loves a two-and-a-half-year-old Bobby climbed over the rails out of his cot in order to kiss little Bobby; he would do anything for him. Our young Scottish red-haired houseman (nicknamed Ginger) pointed out to me how the children with a bad heart breathe differently from normal children and what happens when children are undernourished as is little Georgie, who has not enough white corpuscles, has sores and is so pale. We inject him with Pentide 10cc, but what effect drugs have I don't yet understand. Ginger explained to me the effect of the M and B drug, a new antibiotic. We are giving it to a little boy who had mastoidectomy, to prevent infection.

Before my new friend Mrs Somogyi left the hospital, we had a long talk, and I shall be visiting her. She said that the English wear a serious mask, but are very sensitive underneath. I do agree! She also added that it is a good thing if a queen sits on the throne, because then the state is ruled by her consort. If a king is on the throne, then it is not so good, because then the state is ruled by a woman (as the king listens to his wife, for example, Louis in France)! I suppose that is English humour. Like the saying that the English Channel is too stormy for any shipping to pass, therefore Europe is isolated.

I read in the papers of the persecution of traitors in Czechoslovakia, or rather, how we shall deal with them after the war. I am wondering how the writers of these articles would behave if they were in the situation of the 'traitors'. I also ask how are all those I love at home? How are they withstanding the pressures? Be brave, my parents, be brave, may God bless you and help you. Life is strange, I try to use my head in most situations but am finding out that, without the accompaniment of feelings and heart, using one's head alone is not enough. Anyhow, the most important characteristic I need at present is patience. Patience at work and patience with this war.

Mr Allner's mother had a letter from Cedric and in it he asked after me, hoping that I had news of home. He also sent a food parcel for my birthday. Why am I so very thrilled at his attention? Why so pleased that now I have a good reason to write to him? And why did I dream of my old friend Pepik, who was so poorly clad and in my dream walked past me and I felt so sorry for him? Is the friendship of the past going to turn into love in the future? How are we both changing? What will the future hold? Will I have a future at home? When will that be?

I have decided to share a bedroom with my nursing friend Maskell, and with the matron's consent we have moved to a small one in the attic. The room is basic, but the view is terrific! Over the glorious garden we can see the green park, the waters of the sparkling blue lake, the habitat of ducks and swans and, joy of joys, in the distance the horizon meets the sea. To add to our contentment, we sleep with our windows wide open. We were prohibited to do this on the ground floor.

I read whenever I can, but even when off duty we have to attend lectures and study. When I read *Czechoslovak*, I feel nearer to those at home. Believe me, Father, even though a person is nineteen years old, she would so like to rest her head in your lap and kiss the hands of her Mother. Even to be told off, punished and reprimanded. My very dear English friends are so polite, I really do not know what they think of me and what mistakes I make. It is hard to find out about my failings, but I am trying. I can face anything, do anything, I have so much strength, so much good will, I am not afraid.

After a relaxing break of four days and nights I was back working nights and again in the men's ward, which was overflowing with casualties. There was only nurse Gale and myself to look after everyone. But we felt we were useful, and I was glad that I knew how to help those brave men. When the younger ones made passes at me, and when my heart – so eager to love – wanted to respond, I decided my feelings were just of pity and that any relationship must be strictly friendship. The same rule applied to the young doctors. I had to be free to go home when the time came. I was unable to follow my sister's advice to live for the day:

After all, tomorrow is also a day. That is what I tried to tell Věra. How does one know the difference between love and compassion? Will I know as I grow older?

It is Sunday. I wanted to go to church because the preacher I like, Mr Guillingham, is joining the navy and is leaving us. But I was so sleepy for I am still on night duty. I also felt that it was wrong to go to church only when I feel in need of God, so I decided to pray really well in bed. Oh dear, half-way through my prayer I fell asleep.

D uring our four-year nursing training, we had a number of hospital examinations and 'lectures from a sister tutor and from visiting doctors. After working for two years and passing the hospital exams, we sat a preliminary state examination, and two years later, after four years of nursing, the final state examination declared us State Registered Nurses!

End of February
In a few days we have the doctors' exams. And I am now in charge of the men's ward, which is bulging at the seams. I can cope with all this, but not so with the news that ration books in Czechoslovakia have been taken away from all Jews and they are forbidden to buy unrationed food. What other deprivation do they have to suffer that we are ignorant of?

O nly hard work relieved my despair. I was not going to tell Věra what was happening at home, but they read it in the newspaper at her school:

Yesterday I had a letter from darling Věra, full of tears and panic. So, instead of sleeping and studying, I wrote fourteen pages to her. Not to console her, that is impossible. I tried to help her to carry our burden. I wrote about faith, about courage, how our tears are a little selfish, just an expression of our own pain for they do not help those at home. I mentioned that I work hard and laugh and joke with my patients so as not to let them see that underneath that mask my heart is breaking too. I suggested to my blue-eyed sister that the best way she can help our parents is by studying hard. I did not tell her that Mr Herckza received the news that our granny is dead. She does not need to carry that pain yet. But I did tell her that Mr Herczka had news saying our parents were all right. I omitted to add that this news was sent before the latest newspaper announcement.

My dearest parents, I am unable to describe here for you what is happening in my heart. Such a battle is going on in there, and I, the owner, do not know which side is victorious. Whatever I do, in a way, I do for you. How do you view this life? I take it apart, bit by bit, I try to understand, but it is hard. When is goodness really good and evil really all evil? When is shame complete shame and love, love supreme? Perhaps I should write of my life's philosophy, but I doubt that anyone would wish to read it. Will I ever achieve anything worthwhile? For the time being it suffices that I have enough strength to go to work, then undress and climb into bed. For a long time I have not had the energy even to see my friends, the Allners, who live only ten minutes away.

1.3.1943

I have received another letter full of despair from my sister. Mr Herczka told her about Granny's death. 'I cannot imagine home without her,' she wrote. 'How is Grandad managing and how is Mother bearing this pain?'

I too had thought of all this, yet my tiredness is a kind of balm. But I wrote at once to my dearest Věra. I never knew how hard it was to heal the wounds in one's heart. Compared to that, dealing with wounds inflicted on our bodies is much easier. With the latter you either have tools to help or you don't. In order to console a sad heart that bleeds with pain, one needs something special, an extra gift, I do not know what it is, but I would dearly like to possess it in order to help my sister and in order to help the sick with the wounds we do not see. I try to help Věra to trust in God. My dear father, you said once that people invented God because they are weak and wish to believe that they are more than dust, that their soul is immortal. That they need God for courage to do good. Oh, Father, even if you are right, who is courageous enough to walk the path of life without His help? Who is so good as to do good only without thought of a reward, who so brave as to accept fate's cruelty without hoping for justice later? If there are such people, I do not seem to belong among them.

I tried to explain to my sister that our granny is in heaven, that she is with her youngest son, that the happiness she shares now is far greater than her experiences on earth. Her memory will live for ever in our hearts. I tried to tell Věra that our mother surely knows that the old have to die, that I expect Grandfather is living with Mother, that their strength to carry on lies in their hope of seeing us again. And we must not disappoint them.

At long last, I was back on day duty. For the few days before the change-over I went to the Allners. This time my 'holiday' started by my sleeping non-stop for twenty hours. Their two Canadians, billetted with them, Allan and Terry, were great fun. Apparently Allan sent a letter to his fiancée in Canada saying that he was hungry and would she please send a lobster. He covered nearly three pages just asking for a lobster. When the letter arrived, his fiancée found an enclosed note from the censor saying, 'For God's sake, send it.'

5.3.1943

Three planes crashed into Poole Harbour; two airmen were killed and two are in our hospital. Věra is in and out of love all the time. Would you smile at your younger daughter, Mother and Father? She is a terrific girl, so sensible and so brave, and studying hard. You would be proud of her if you saw her school report. I hope you would be proud of me as well, because I have passed all of my hospital exams really well. I love you so much, my dearest parents.

At one of our dances I met an airman from Scotland called Bill. He is very nice and knows so much about my country. And at long last I have saved enough money to buy a bicycle for nine pounds. I feel so free, to be able to cycle wherever I wish.

Our Mr Smith, who is a patient here, speaks to me only in Latin! My lessons at home come in handy, I can understand him. Mr Smith gave me a book about Poole, which he had written.

And more good news: We have a new houseman who is Czech. Honza Pacovsky is quite a bit older than the others, has brown hair, which is already turning grey, but it is curly. He has large dark eyes and is also Jewish. He avoids talking about the past, but it is wonderful to discourse in Czech. What is this strange tie between countrymen?

I also had eleven pages from my sister, who had spent a few days in Edinburgh and enjoyed every moment of it:

Věra sounds well and happy again, I do wish she could always be so. While on my bicycle, I met the ex-patient Roy, we cycled for twenty miles and walked for six miles in the New Forest . . .

I have met Roy again. We cycled, talked and explored this beautiful countryside. Would you object, Mother and Father? And what about you, Pepik? How faithful should I be to a childhood friendship, which, as I grow, appears to become more than friendship? Shall we understand each other again? Shall we find a meeting ground? Are you alive? What kind of a person have you become? Oh, this war that plunged me from the bosom of my family into England's green and pleasant land! Will it ever end?

The month of March was still with us when I read in the papers of Nazi extermination camps, and of the inhuman conditions of these concentration camps into which Jews were herded. Unable to grasp the full horror of what I had read, I kept repeating to myself, 'Not our parents, not our parents.' I continued to work as if my brain was numbed. Then a film about a Czech town called Terezín was shown in England. This medieval fortress town was cleared of its Aryan population and was now entirely Jewish. The film we saw was made in Germany in order to show the rest of the world how well Hitler treated the Jews and that the stories of concentration camps were just a myth. Jews were not tortured, they were not being massacred. Because of the war there was overcrowding in Terezín, but people were content, children attended schools, Jewish doctors worked in hospitals and Jewish artists performed plays and concerts in the theatres. There were synagogues within the wall of this ghetto, people were leading normal lives.

It was easier for the free world to believe what this film depicted rather than the harrowing stories told by the few who had escaped from the concentration camps. I did not know then that Terezín was a township where people were 'sorted out'. Those of mixed marriages were left behind to die of cold, hunger and disease. Yet their chance of survival was far greater than those taken to concentration camps or to the gas chambers of Auschwitz.

I did not know then that my Father had made a private deal with an Aryan friend who, on paper only, took over Father's business. As a Jew, Father was ordered to hand over his business to the Germans. A collaborator in our town reported Father's action to the Gestapo. As a result, Father and his friend were taken to 'Little Fortress' in Terezín, which was turned into a dreaded Gestapo prison not shown on the German propaganda film. Few prisoners came out alive from these dungeons after suffering unspeakable treatment from Nazi hands.

Nor did I know till I had her letter full of despair that my sister and her schoolmates saw the film about Terezín and heard the talk of concentration camps. Again I tried to put aside my pain and fear and summon enough wisdom in a letter to carry courage to my sister. Věra has kept that letter to this day. She wrote back to say, 'I read your letter many times. It helped not only me but many of my friends who have no kind, big sister to turn to.' The following extracts are from that letter:

... One thing I have learnt, my darling Věra, in most cases when we grieve and weep we feel sorry for ourselves. You are shedding tears because you cannot imagine life without our parents. Just think how much greater would be their suffering if they knew of your unhappiness. And, my dearest, if the very worst was to happen, isn't there enough time for grieving?

My patients call me 'a smiler'. I smile at them for they also have reasons for shedding tears. My love for our mother and father is as strong as yours – with each passing year it seems to grow stronger. I, too, cannot imagine our home without their loving presence. All our hopes and struggles are centred on us being with them again. That can never change. We have to live and work and try to be happy, even if their gaze follows us from heaven. Were that to be the case, our parents would be so very close to us, and we must never let them down.

I know that you, my brave sister, understand. I never wanted to mention to you the possibility that our family might not live to see the end of the war. I can only beg of you, live and do not grieve. Try to be happy. You say that all your endeavours are centred on them, so be happy for them. Have faith and be patient . . .

I knew that I had a very courageous sister, who was known not only for her good looks but also for her kind heart. I also knew that in her school everyone feared for parents and other relatives. I fervently hoped that sharing their grief would help them to bear their pain.

My fears for those at home were shared by Honza, the Czech doctor, as well as Mrs Frank and Rita Somogyi. Rita was close to me in age, and I adored her baby, Andrew:

I am so fortunate to be able to discuss everything with three countrymen. But even to them I find it hard to express all my feelings. Mrs Frank treats me like a daughter in a way! I like this.

One of the many ex-patients whom I used to visit was 'Granny' Saunders. She was a delightful old lady, living in Corfe Castle, a charming Dorset village that often welcomed me and my bicycle. And so did 'my' granny, in her little flat, whose windows spied on the feet of passing pedestrians:

Coming here is like coming to another world. When Granny's son presented her with a vacuum cleaner I found her sweeping the floor after using it. Just in case! My granny thought the new gadget was untrustworthy.

No matter when I arrived, no matter how busy she was in her shop next to the flat, out of beautiful china I would receive my cup of tea. Home-made cakes were never missing from the table.

Inevitably on my bicycle rides, I was accompanied by Roy.

I MUST NOT LOVE YOU

Roy became my constant companion. The meningitis he caught while in the air force left with him a slight limp and half of his face was numb. For a while Roy had to wear a little chain to hold his lip up, causing his speech to slur slightly. Tall, fair haired and blue eyed, Roy felt a little embarrassed by what he considered to be his deficiencies. I well remember how reluctantly he came to a restaurant with me. Brought together by our love of open space, of walking, cycling and swimming, our affection for each other grew. His love for me was complete, real and true. I felt it, needed it and it filled a void in my heart – the great longing for the love of my parents. With all my being I was eager to return this loving; yet I refused to give in to this natural inclination:

I must not love you so, I must be free to return home after the war to my parents and perhaps to Pepik.

I told Roy we must remain friends only, and I begged him to help me because I find it difficult to stick to principles. Roy agreed, and we shall continue a loving friendship, for we do enjoy each other's company. I feel as if I have imprisoned my heart in a cage and told it not to beat freely. Is this what you would ask of me, my dearest mother and father? My thinking is muddled as my feelings interfere too much. I suggested to Roy that we split up, for I do not wish to hurt him. He begged me to stay and said, 'I love you so much. I know how you feel and I shall respect your feelings. I cannot deny that I hope you may allow yourself to love me freely one day, but in the meantime let us enjoy our time together.'

And we did.

July 1943
Roy has kissed me. The night was beautiful, the stars shimmering in the sky, with the rays of a large moon laughing in our faces. We stood on the cliffs watching the sparkling waters as the waves rolled and rolled without ceasing. And then it happened. You would understand, wouldn't you, Mother and Father? It is not that I love you less, Roy and I will remain just friends. It is not easy, and I do not wish to plunder his heart and run away with it. There are so many different kinds of loving.

I am writing a day later. Our tutor asked today if we are studying hard.

Everyone said 'yes', only my 'no' came loud and clear! I really should study instead of reading. The book in my hand is called *The Christ of The Indian Road* by Stanley Jones. It tries to show that it is Christ only (not the Christian religion, which has too many different meanings) who can overcome the world. The author argues this because India wants Christ and his teaching without having to embrace Western civilization as well.

10.7.1943

Today we invaded Sicily; in spite of this, it is being said the war will have to be suffered for another three years. Maybe after this we shall invade the Balkan states, or maybe start the second front in the west. Somehow I do not wish to write about the war in here. The history of it will be recorded in history books far more accurately. But God, please, let us see the end soon.

I have sold one of my dresses from home, the grey one. It was in perfect condition, but too small for me. With it went some of my love; I could see my darling mother, how she so carefully packed all our possessions, trying to hide the tears in her eyes. Now we need cloth coupons to buy clothes, these do not allow for extravagance. So I am glad that a nurse appreciated my dress.

Today I have written to Mrs Rainford, Mr Herczka and Miss Vinall. Roy is having a week's holiday in Devon, and I keep getting cards. My forthcoming holiday will be spent with Věra. I am so eager to see her again. I am so proud of her. Fifteen years old. I remember what it felt like to be fifteen. It is a pity that those years can never return.

My free time was shared between the Allners and Roy. I remember being very amused when we cut thin sandwiches for afternoon tea at the tennis club frequented by Mrs Allner and Bunty. Such very thin sandwiches were unknown in my country. Besides that, the look of the loaf once I finished with it does not bear description, it resembled a steep slope! My sandwich cutting never improved.

Another 'very English' habit left me perplexed, for I had never watched cricket before. All these men in white, whatever were they doing? The first game I watched was with Roy. He tried to explain, but to this day I have not grasped the intricacies of this famous game.

I went with my family, the Allners, to the little Anglican church whenever possible. I could not sing, and unfortunately for those around me I did enjoy the hymn singing.

I have been discussing Christianity with Mrs Allner. She stressed that Jesus Himself said He came not to destroy the Old Testament, but to fulfil it.

In the papers was a very good article written by the Archbishop of Canterbury. He was writing about the increasing dishonesty in the world.

'To hold on to the old English honesty is most important,' he said, 'To aspire to be the most that man can be, not to sink to the lowest denominator in men's nature. To work for peace is important, but is not everything. We also have to live in a way which would make us worthy of the peace we crave.'

This England; sometimes I feel so close to her people and sometimes so far away. But, with all her faults and all her virtues, one cannot but love this land.

M y sister spent her school holidays partly in London, partly in a Guide camp in Scotland and partly in Lancashire where I joined her. Boys also now played a great part in her life.

I travelled from Poole to Ainsdale, which was about a ten-hour journey in those days, with two changes of train. My heart was racing when I saw my sister at the station. She was more grown up than when I last saw her and so pretty. Mr and Mrs Rainford and Dorothy welcomed me as if I was another member of the family, but as soon as we finished our evening meal Věra and I cycled to the sea:

For some reason we needed to be in the fresh air and together. We talked in our bed most of the night, there was so much to tell. Letters are a very poor substitute.

Věra is fifteen now and in love with Vernon. She told me, 'Eva, I am so in love with him, but I mustn't see him so much and take it too seriously.' I remembered Pepik and knew how she was feeling. Then Věra added, 'Do you think our parents would be angry?'

I thought that no matter what we do, no matter what we talk about, Mother and Father are always present. I share with Věra the little of life's wisdom that I can grasp, so I replied, 'As long as you behave so that you do not need to be ashamed in front of yourself, Mother and Father would not chastise you. After all, this half childish, half adult love is one of the purest among sexes. I shall never regret being fond of Pepik.'

I am so glad that my sister and I can discuss everything. Would you approve of my comments to her, my dear ones? After all, there would have been no point in forbidding her anything. A youthful heart finds its way in spite of all difficulties.

We also talked about religion. Věra said, 'Aren't we all children of God as Christ is?' I had no answer, I don't know the Bible well.

T he next day we went to stay with Mr and Mrs Campion, Věra's second home. Again I received a warm welcome and was accepted as if I had not been away. Věra and I found the frequent church-going a little difficult:

97

On Sunday we went to church in the morning, and the rest of the day Věra and I spent walking and talking. Mrs Campion wanted us to go to church in the evening too, but perhaps the Almighty is satisfied with one visit. Věra and I had so much to discuss . . . I was disappointed in her when she told me that she does not mention Vernon's kisses in her diary; after all, everything has to be written there honestly for our parents.

T he fourteen days with my sister were going far too fast. We visited Desmond's parents and met Desmond himself, now in a naval uniform, looking very handsome and in love with a young girl. Though I had rejected him, was it jealousy that I felt?

Mr and Mrs Campion's daughter, Moyra, was to be married shortly and Věra was to be her bridesmaid. We spent evenings reading each other's old letters from our parents and friends at home. I never travelled without them, and at night they stayed in a little bag under my bed. The Nazi bombs might destroy everything around me, but not this treasure that was more precious than anything else. I was amused by what I thought to be a very English habit:

Here the bus conductors sometimes have children in their charge. When the bus stops they take the child by the hand and walk across the road with him or her while the passengers have to wait. The buses also stop if there are any dogs lying in the road and wait for them to move. The same thing happens if there is a kitten or a cow. Oh, England!

I had a lovely letter from Roy. Of one thing I am sure, Roy understands me so well. I feel his love and know of my affection for him. I am so confused, my emotions zig-zag, I wish we could return to Czechoslovakia now. I feel myself changing, I am learning a great deal in a foreign land and yet I know how very little I do know. If I had a stronger faith, would I know better how to live? I so long for the feeling of pure joy I used to know at home, just for a moment, to ease this heaviness that never seems to leave me.

26.7.1943

Mussolini has resigned. Martial law has been declared in Italy. We are bombing Germany. I am glad, but with this feeling of relief is mingled sadness for all those who lose their loved ones, wherever they may be. So many people are hurt, so many killed, so many are giving up hope and faith. And the English are still very serious about their golf and cricket!

A s always, I was sad when leaving friends, but leaving Věra was hardest, though I knew that she was happy. On my way home I spent a few hours in London with Mr Herczka, and felt that I had hurt his feelings when I laughed at his remark, 'You should marry in England and give up nursing, the work is far too hard for you.' I was never robust.

Yet, we all had a great deal of energy. After work during summer time, when it stayed light to about 11pm, I often played tennis with other nurses and doctors until darkness compelled us to go to bed. Roy did not play tennis, but he was a steadfast and true friend. When I worried about the hurt I would surely inflict when I eventually disappeared from his horizon to return home, he would reply, 'I shall not think about that now.'

Our relationship is like a tug of war. Roy pulls me to him and I pull away, for I must find out what has happened to Pepik before I feel free to love elsewhere. I told Roy, 'I am mad, I do not want to hurt the boy in Czechoslovakia, but I do not want to nor am I able to give you up.'

We lived on our bicycles. Were there any lanes in Dorset unknown to Roy and me? Whenever we were free, we cycled for miles and miles. I vividly remember one evening when the red light on my bike fell off and smashed on the roadside. I was lucky, in my bag I carried red lipstick, given me by Allan, the Canadian. Lipstick was unavailable in those days. Although I never used make-up, I carried this to feel more grown up! That evening the lipstick was used to redden grease-proof paper taken from around our sandwiches. We then tied the paper around the naked bulb.

The five-bedroom house of the Allners billeted many men from the forces at various times. There was plenty of company for dances and going to the cinema with others besides Roy, but to the latter I always returned. The greatest love Věra and I knew was far away, we were thirsty and grateful for any affection that reached us. Yet I felt I did not have the freedom to return it completely to Roy.

I spoke in Czech with Honza Pacovsky, our Czech houseman, and we talked about home. Nowhere in my diary do I mention why he was at our hospital and why he was there for such a short time. But I do remember that he was very serious:

Honza and I share our fears for those at home. He has a fiancée in Prague. But we talk mostly about our patients and England, neither of us finds it easy to discuss the inner pain. We also agree that some characteristics are typically English. I told him of a conversation I had with another nurse who accused the Russians of coming into the war only to save their own skin. When I retorted that the English had done the same, she simply agreed! I expected her to be angry with me. There is something nice about the English, who do not seem to have this constant need to defend themselves and can laugh at themselves.

O ne of my duties included working in the out-patients section of the psychiatric department:

Dr Hornsby looks right through me with his eyes; I have this feeling when he looks at me that he can read my every thought with his penetrating look. As for Dr Stables, he has only one leg, but is very nice. But he is so deaf. I have to call his patients into the room and then write down for him what they say! It is hard work. When, to excuse some mistakes I made, I told him that I was from Czechoslovakia he was extra pleasant to me, and asked if I would be helping him next week. Such is this England.

October
Věra writes often and I am so happy that she confides in me. She is seeing Vernon and is still in love with him; one can follow one's sense and heart only. I know that it is hard to forget the one who gave the first kiss.

My sister was also troubled because a schoolmate accused her of cowardice for having been baptized. So at once I wrote back something to the effect that: you were too young for anyone to be able to blame you for what happened. Our parents were baptized because they loved us and were hoping this action might ease or even prevent our suffering. We were never practising Jews and we always mixed with and lived among Christians. Maybe England will instil in us a Christian faith. That does not mean that we would not pray for all the Jews or be ashamed that we belong to the Jewish race. Anyhow, God is the only one who is Father of us all, no matter what our religion. He understands the complexities and He will help. I could not explain more for I do not understand myself.

L ife was full, my duties in the out-patient department finished and I was working again in the children's ward:

It is hard work, but also fun. When Roland was recovering from his anaesthetic he called all the doctors lunatics. Yet when his eyes fell on the pretty face of my friend Ann he exclaimed, 'Hello darling.' Kids! They all want to be kissed, but not all are 'kissable' with their runny noses and spotty faces. One night the older boys demanded that I sing to them in Czech. When I finished my song, Derek turned to me saying, 'But, nurse, one day you will really sing, won't you?'

The boys can say 'thank you', 'please', 'good evening', etc., in Czech. I was demonstrating to Honza Pacovsky how clever they are. Honza says he is missing me in the out-patients.

Someone brought bananas for the children, most of them have never seen any, and little Maggie refused to have a bit of this strange food. I shall also remember with joy little seven-year-old Peter from the Crippled Children's Home who, when having a bath, is like a jellyfish and can neither sit nor talk. When I was drying him he started hitting my hand. I pretended to cry. He took my hand and kissed it. I gathered him up in my arms and he kissed my face. I hugged him tight and felt so happy. Why were my eyes wet?

But we had to laugh when we heard one boy say to another, 'Are you medical or surgical?'

'What do you mean?'

'I mean, were you bad when they brought you here or did they make you bad when you came?'

There are also children who do not joke and children who die in our ward; I am learning about life and death, and at times I remember having written to my parents that I shall keep my rose-tinted spectacles on my eyes. It is hard to see the world through rose-coloured spectacles when events around you prove that life is mostly grey. Only a child can ignore this, and I am no more a child.

It is also hard to watch any of my children die, and good to see them go home well again. Seven-year-old Norman's mother phoned me begging me to come to their home and talk to Norman, who was refusing to go to school. After finding out Norman's aspirations in life, and talking about them, and telling him that without schooling he will achieve nothing, Norman trotted off to school as long as I walked with him to the gate. I think at times it is easier for a comparative stranger than for a mother to 'manage' a child.

For the first time I was made to feel a foreigner here, when our home Sister Thomas reprimanded me for having a tear in my apron. As I was very busy, I asked for permission to change the garment later. Permission was not granted and sister added, 'You must be clean and tidy like the English nurses.' I was hurt and furious and so were my nursing friends when I told them.

The Prime Minister, Winston Churchill, knew how to give courage and hope, though at the start of the war he promised us nothing but toil. In November 1943, on Lords Mayor Day, when the new Lord Mayor of London was elected, Churchill's speech included a reminder that before peace could be won many tears would have to be shed because many more lives would be lost. Churchill also added that we, who stood alone in 1940, would be victorious. In 'my' hospital the patients as well as the staff always listened to his speeches.

I tried to break up with Roy, for I feel he deserves someone better than me, someone without my problems. Someone who would make him happier, who does not carry a ghost of home and Pepik. Roy begged me not to part, saying that no one can make him happier. So we carry on.

Věra gave me a real telling off, she wrote, 'Stop thinking about Pepik, who knows what has happened to him? Others also have to leave their future to an unknown fate.'

Then Věra wrote that she does not get on well with the girls in her class, there is much squabbling and what should she do. 'What are we fighting for when even a handful of Czech girls cannot live together?' she asked. So I tried to help and also told her not to lose her sense of proportion. Churchill said that in one of his speeches.

I have also written to three boys in the forces, at different times they were billeted with the Allners. They are friendly letters, to cheer them up. I have no idea where they are or if they will return. So many lives have been lost, so writing is the least I can do – and knitting socks and scarves. Mrs Allner told me that she feels I have been put into this world in order to cheer up others and bring them comfort! If only I knew how. But it was nice of her to say so. In the midst of this war, I really am fortunate.

I even sang and whistled as I returned through the park to my hospital, for it was Poole Park with its two lakes that divided the hospital from the Allner's house. Busy but happy at work, surrounded by friends, studying hard for more hospital exams, the past ceased to overpower the present and some of the heaviness I carried eased. I was almost happy. But not for long.

DON'T YOU THINK, GOD, THAT I HAVE ENOUGH ON MY PLATE?

T owards the end of November 1943 I had a letter from Mr Herczka. It read:

'I had news from my friend in Stockholm. Your parents and Auntie Berta are in Terezín. My friend had sent them packets of food.'

Then Mr Herczka asked me to send him a sponge for washing as he was unable to get one in London.

I did remember his request a few days later, but on this day I felt crushed. Till now I had hoped that our dear ones had managed to remain in their home, and had escaped deportation.

Why, God, why? Oh, my mother and father, how I wish I could help you. Not knowing how you are is a torture. And to think that I was living a life of comparative ease. Every moment that I have laughed since I left you is a reproach to me. Every bit of happiness I have felt is saying to me, 'You have enjoyed life whilst your parents were suffering.'

My dearest ones, I do hope that one day I shall be able to make it all up to you, take care of you. I know now that nothing will be the same when we return, that we shall have to give comfort to you and Auntie. Our home may not be there, but please *live*. I'll be brave, I'll work hard, I shall not let you down. And I will do all I can to make sure Věra is happy, I am not going to tell her of your fate just now, the sunshine of our lives must not shed tears.

I could not hold back my tears when I told Mrs Allner, she gave me strength by saying to me, 'Your courage will help you through.' I had to go back to work, but could not remove a picture from my mind: a picture of my parents being ill treated and suffering.

As soon as I was free, I wrote to Mr Herczka asking him not to send such bitter news to Věra. Why should she be made unhappy when she cannot do anything? To her I wrote a cheerful letter and sent her all my sweet ration for this month. Then I wrote to Cedric and Allan for Christmas. After that I was so exhausted that even my intense fear for those at home did not keep me awake.

Later I heard that I could send food parcels to Terezín via the Red Cross; at least I could do something to help. But could it harm my parents in some way, bring repercussions upon their heads? Again I ventured to write to President Beneš, this time asking for advice. My letter was answered by his secretary, and the comments helped me to decide to send a third of my monthly salary each month for food parcels. I begged God to make sure that this would help and not harm my parents. Later I wrote:

This morning the rain came down in buckets but I chose to go on foot to the Allner's house. I think better when walking in the rain!

Bunty's parents invited Věra to spend Christmas with them, so that we could be together during my free hours. As I walked, in front of me I imagined I could see my sister arriving in her new coat and dress, given to her by Mrs Campion. Here was a pretty girl looking at the world through rose-coloured glasses – as I used to once upon a time – full of self-confidence and, like most sixteen year olds, assured of her popularity. I don't ever want to harm Věra, I love her dearly, but I visualized myself next to her in my ancient coat with my unruly hair, I saw my tired face next to her bright one, my dark brown eyes forever searching and full of pain next to her sparkling blue eyes. Something hurt a little. Not because I am jealous of her, God forbid, but because I am not like her. After all, my eyes too used to be full of mischief. Suddenly I realized that how we look is largely dependent on our character. Bad temper, selfishness and meanness look at the world through our eyes. Faith and joy beautify our countenance. Happiness glows in people's eyes. That is why youth is wonderful.

The rain on my face witnessed my joyful smile. Everything depends on us alone. A coat will not alter our nature, but our nature will alter our countenance. My dearest Věra, stay as you are – a happy child. The day of our reunion with Mother and Father is drawing closer. They will not look at our coats, they will gaze into our eyes looking for joy and laughter. Both of us are so much theirs – yet my heart is heavy with fear for them.

Věra arrived, she was already a well-developed young woman. Our relationship was changing, the age difference was growing smaller. Yet I still felt responsible and eager to protect her from any harm.

I had postponed the ordeal of telling Věra of our parents' fate until one evening after Christmas Day. Then I tried gently to convey the sad news I had learnt a few weeks earlier. We shared our fear, we shared our grief and our hopes. Both of us begged God for mercy for the parents we loved. Věra was half expecting to hear such news, which eased the shock for her. Our friends made sure that this Christmas holiday was happy for us. And, in spite of all the pain and worry, it was a happy Christmas.

By now I was working in the X-ray department learning the intricacies of the machines. There was many a night when I was hauled out of bed for accidents or to stand with my gadget in the theatre during an operation. There was no time to make up for lost sleep the next day, for I longed to spend all my free time with my sister. Never before and never since were we as close to each other as we were during the war years, even when distance separated us. Though always thinking about home, always fearing for those at home, both our lives were full. By now I was almost permanently tired:

I don't know why I am so tired, but it is not a physical tiredness because Watch and I ran to the shop where we queued to get dog meat. And I managed to buy six lemons — I have not seen those since the war began.

Everyone says that 1944 should see us victorious at long last. My dearest parents, I think of you so much, I so look forward to seeing you. Are we going to understand each other as before? Am I going to be as much yours as I was in the past? Of course, I am only yours. And what about you, Pepik? What do you do? How do you view life? Please, God, protect my dearest ones, You are the only one who can help.

T he birth of 1944 spelt the departure of 1943, the year that heralded victories for the Allies at El Alamein and later at Stalingrad. Until then the Allies had suffered many defeats, from now on the course of the war turned. Later we read that at least one third of Berlin was destroyed in air-raids. My reaction is voiced in my journal:

I know that we can win this war only by destroying the Germans before they destroy us. I would fight for you, give my life for you, my dearest ones, but how will fighting and hatred cease if we forget the magic of forgiveness? We shall have to prove to the defeated that we can achieve more by peaceful means than in war. Out of the heart of every individual in the world, the feeling of hatred must disappear. That will be so very hard, I know, but without this how can peace prevail?

I am reading My Son My Son by Howard Spring. He provides a number 'of thoughts that impress me: 'Love for the same things never makes allies, it's always hatred that does it,' but, '. . . when you finish, what have you left between yourselves? Hatred only;' 'God damn every country which sacrifices one young life to reach its glory;' '. . . in pride and blindness we told the fate what to do with our sons'. This was said by a broken-hearted father upon hearing of the death of his son. I agree, but how do we deal with aggressors like Hitler?

I failed the practical part of my preliminary nursing exam as I misunderstood the examiner, and I was not permitted to remedy this when clarification dawned on me. But I passed the hardest part, anatomy, physiology and hygiene, with flying colours. This was not enough:

God, I know that there are far worse things happening in the world, but do You not think that for someone who has always reached her goal, this is quite a heavy blow? I know I was worried and could not concentrate well, but I do not want to disappoint my parents, and I so wish to finish my training by the time this war is over so that I can help those at home. Don't You think, God, that without this I have enough on my plate to feel bitter towards life? I know I am young and strong, but even still, I could do with some encouragement. Oh, I am mad. I am not really complaining, God Almighty. You do know why You do whatever You do. Everything is in Your hands.

January 1944
The hospital dances are more frequent now, about once every six weeks. Five airmen asked me for a date at the last one, as this was before my forthcoming exam I refused everyone.

Sometimes I think that with the best of intentions I really am very silly. Still, even silly people are human. I try to be good, but it is hard to be so all the time. Honza has gone to another hospital, I miss him.

15 January
The Russians are in Poland. But they do not seem to get on with each other, and the English have to intercede. Everybody talks about the 'Curzon Line'. I do hope all will end well.

Yesterday one of the doctors said to me, 'Aren't you lucky to be here.'

My answer was, 'I shall not be sure about that until after the war is over. Anyone can run away.'

'Don't be silly,' he replied angrily, 'there you could do nothing, here you are performing a valuable task.' I hope he is right, and that those at home will see it in the same light. If I was home now, would I be full of hatred or would I understand what I only dimly grasp about the destructive power of hate?

When I look through my diaries I wonder if I am not wasting time randomly writing my thoughts and activities. Life is strange, like a jigsaw puzzle. We look for the pieces and think the picture is nearly complete, but it never ends. Ours is not to know the answer to the perplexity of life.

March

Back in the men's ward we are busy as always. I want to clean out Cedric's boat in my free time, the nearest I get to sailing without him, and spend some time with Roy on our bikes. We pick primroses, bluebells and daffodils, my bicycle basket often overflows with this glory of spring. The aroma does not just fill my bedroom for I share their beauty with Trixie, Gempie, Ann, Mary and other nursing friends. Last evening we again supplemented our diet with fish and chips, eating them in the long corridor and talking non-stop. How is it that we never run out of topics for conversation?

I n the spring of 1944 Bunty married Noel. They radiated happiness and joy. I thought them a perfect pair, she so pretty and petite, he tall, dark and handsome in his air force uniform. The sun was smiling on their great day, witnessing their love and delight. Bunty followed Noel to Scotland. I attempted to fill the void left by her departure in her parents' lives, though I too missed my friend.

As the days of 1944 advanced, so did the Allied armies. The Russians were in the Eastern part of Czechoslovakia. I wrote to the Czech Red Cross in London offering my services. Their reply was plain and simple: as your final exams are only a few months ahead, finish your training first. Then you will be of real assistance.

In October, Arnhem in Holland was occupied by the British, Tito took over Belgrade, and General Rommel died. The end of the war was truly in sight.

Honza Pacovsky came to visit me, for he was to be among the first to be repatriated home when the time came. As a doctor his help was needed. We talked, hoped, made plans. Well aware that the real future might bear little resemblance to the one we hoped for.

My diary is all about me, is this what you asked of me, my dearest father? On paper I am presenting your daughter to you. I know that you and Mother will forgive my many failings. You will read about my joys and my pain, about my despair, my hope and my faith. You will read about my thoughts, faults, ignorance, problems and battles. About my love for my patients, young and old, and for my many friends of both sexes. And for my bicycle – one of my greatest joys is to speed on a country lane with the wind in my hair and sometimes rain on my face. Life is full, I am so rich, yet without you so poor.

B y Christmas 1944 there was no doubt that the end of the cruel war was nigh. Cedric was in India, having survived battles in Burma, and was to come home shortly. Hospital parties and dances were seized with a new excitement, the feeling that the coming year would bring peace to the world pervaded all thoughts:

Is this my last Christmas in England? Do I dare to hope? I have received thirty-six presents from friends and patients; though I gave many myself, this amount left me amazed. I was also well endowed with gifts on the first of January, my twenty-first birthday. New Year's Day, another day. What will it bring?

Though he wished the fulfilment of my dream, Roy could not but be sad:

Roy whispered today, 'When you are home, remember always that you have made one Englishman very happy.' Dear Roy, I hope he will not regret knowing me.

The snow has fallen and the Poole lakes are frozen. I went skating. I had to go alone, as none of my friends knows how to skate.

The Russians are forty-five miles from Berlin, where are you my dear ones? Věra is in love with Walter, a boy in her school. We are so busy, we cannot remember what it feels like not to be tired. Working in the theatre means that we have to get up at night for emergencies. This does not entitle us to stay in bed the next morning.

I had a really happy birthday and am so looking forward to telling you all about it, Mother and Father. Here I will write the poem that my Big Man composed for me. Isn't it wonderful?

A line to you, dear Eva, since you are twenty-one today,
A grown up woman now, though dwelling still neath foreign skies;
Yet faithful to your homeland as the day you went away.
(The case with those who are good and true could not be otherwise.)

Some years have passed since you and Věra set out for this shore;
You came in faith, a trust conveyed by those you hold most dear;
It was brave of them; 'twas best for you we hope and furthermore
Your sojourn's brought much brightness to your friends who love you here.

We are glad you like our country and we are glad you now belong
To woman's noblest calling – aiding those who are maimed or ill;
But may the years to come for you be filled with happy song
At home again; God bless you dear;
*   yet – think of England still.*

B unty's and Noel's happiness was shortlived; two days after my birthday Noel was killed in an air accident. Bunty returned home to live and give birth, a few months later, to her son. Knowing of my friend's agony, I admired her fortitude. My heart bled for her and I cried for her, but found it hard to express what I really felt:

Bunty is so brave, her one consolation is that Noel did not suffer and that the seven months with him were perfection itself. She firmly believes that they will meet again. I feel so dreadfully sorry for this family and to Bunty I whispered, 'You are a great wife of a great man, God bless you.' But I did not cry until I met Roy, then I could not hold back my tears any longer. Who was it that wrote, 'Better to have loved and lost than never to have loved at all?'

I feel so sad. Please, God, bless Bunty, may her great faith in You be her strength. Bless the Allners who say, 'Thy will be done,' and please, please look after my parents, Pepik and also after Věra, make her happy. As for me, please help me to be better than I am, grant me faith in You and faith in myself.

I felt so strange when I saw Noel's coffin. Suddenly I was overwhelmed by a sudden pang of fear – fear for my parents. It was a strange premonition that I tried hurriedly to dismiss. What silly thoughts.

Of all the people in England except for Věra, it is the Allner family that I love the most, and I wish so much that they did not have to suffer. My love for you, Mother and Father, my fear for you has not diminished my feeling of compassion for them.

I was asked to tidy up the little room that is mine in Bunty's house. There, in the midst of a great muddle, I sat on the floor reading my old letters from my parents and Pepik. I felt so near to my home. You had written, Pepik, that you can love no one but me. I wonder where you are, and I wonder what you are thinking and feeling now six years later. And you Father, you once said that you would forgive us anything; would you still be proud of your two daughters? And you, my dearest mother, your love shines at me out of every line.

WHY, GOD, WHY?

In January 1945 we heard that Terezín would soon be liberated. At once I wrote to the Czech Red Cross begging for information:

Is it possible to find out if our parents are still in Terezín? If so, may we write to them? Could I take my final nursing exam in Czechoslovakia and go home as soon as possible?

To all those questions the answer was in the negative. I cried. Later we heard that 12,000 of the 60,000 inhabitants from Terezín were moved to Switzerland. Again, on writing to the Red Cross I was told that there were no names given of the survivors. They asked me to be patient. Věra and I were in touch constantly. It was hard to find time for my diary, yet I had to finish my task:

Věra isn't certain whether she wants to return home, but feels it her duty to do so. For me it will be the culmination of all my desires – or am I deceiving myself? The home of my birth versus the home of my deliverance, one cannot but be torn. I am lucky to have my sister who understands.

The Russians are in Slovakia.

Cedric has written home that my letter was the one which told him of the death of Noel. 'She put it so nicely,' he wrote. I was pleased, I do have a very soft spot for Ced.

I cannot stop reading poetry, but must study.

In May, Brno, a town in Czechoslovakia, was taken by the Russians:

The Germans in Northern Italy have given up. Berlin has fallen. They say Hitler is dead and Mussolini has been shot. Apparently Goering has committed suicide, only Goebbels may still be alive. The Czech minister of foreign affairs, Jan Masaryk, is in San Francisco. Rita Somogyi and I were discussing everything, she will probably stay in England. Her home is here now. Shortly she will move to London with her baby, Andrew. I have never met her husband, who is in the forces.

110

My friend Ann is crying. At the age of sixteen she had a boyfriend who was taken prisoner two years ago. Ann had no news of him. Now he has returned, is sick and wants to get engaged. Ann is already engaged to another whom she loves. So she is at a loss to know what to do. Poor Ann. We keep talking it over, but only she can decide. With joy yet with apprehension I think of reunion with you, Pepik.

8.5.1945

The midnight clock is chiming. Official VE day. *The war is ended.* I can only whisper, 'Thank You, thank You. Bless them, oh, God, bless my parents, my people, please bless this whole world.' . . .

I can work, but concentrate I cannot. We are trying to trace our parents, Věra's school is supplied with a great deal of information, but where are you my dearest?

23.5.1945

I am in Llanwrtyd Wells, where Věra's school was moved to, spending a week with Věra. You will be as proud of your daughter as I am of my sister, Mother and Father. Her Czech school is as an oasis, here I feel at home. I must not regret that three years ago I did not stay. After all, I did spend those years helping others, though it was hard sometimes; my heart is not as kind as is the heart of my mother.

V ěra and I were very close, sharing our hopes, diminishing each other's fears. I was left breathless by the beauty of the hills and valleys spilling for miles around us. Learning in this environment, among her own people, it was no wonder Věra thrived. Our week together passed far too quickly; we were never to be this close again.

On my return I found a letter from Mr Herczka saying I could write to friends in Czechoslovakia. I am doing so, to Pepik, to others – just a short letter asking: 'How are you? Where are our parents?' Who knows if any of them will receive my notes.

1.6.1945

Věra telephoned. Mother and Auntie Berta are in Belsen Concentration Camp. They are alive! But no one knows where Father is. I am incredibly happy to know that Mother and Auntie are alive. Just now I am refusing even to think of what they must have been through. But my dearest father, my grey-haired friend, where is he? What is he doing? I shall travel to London tomorrow and see if I can find out more from the Red Cross. Inundated with questions, they now take too long to answer letters. Roy will come with me, much to Mrs Allner's relief. I feel she fears for me in case the news is bad. Mother and Father, I think of you, I pray for you, I am only yours.

3.6.1945

The queue at the Red Cross was endless, and they closed before I had a chance to talk to anyone. When, an hour later, Mr Herczka welcomed me at his little flat, he assured me that the Red Cross could give me no new information about Father, as he himself had been in touch and received all news, and that my mother and Auntie will be all right now as they are in the hands of the British.

The visit to Mr Herczka made the journey worthwhile, he was so pleased to see me. Looking older than I expected (he is seventy-four years old), he appears to be a broken man. And he is ill. He is sure my country will not want a German-speaking Jew. I wish he could enjoy the warmth of the sun, song of the birds, children's laughter, these are not the prerogative of any nation. I'll send him some food and buy him a jumper with my coupons. Perhaps then he will cease to be angry with me for not marrying an Englishman and staying in England. He is also angry with my parents for choosing to stay in Czechoslovakia, for feeling more Czech than Jewish, and not escaping when the possibility was there.

Věra sent a letter to me to send on to our parents. It was such a wonderful letter, I copied some of it:

Dearest Mother and Father,

I do not know if either of you will receive this letter. I do not know if Father is still alive, but I am writing to both of you hoping that one of you will read this. If by any chance you are at home, Father, then I am telling you that we had news from Auntie Berta that she and Mother are in Belsen and are alive!

My dearest, I love you so much and I am so looking forward to coming home. Whether both of you or only one of you are there, we want to return, but we hope to find both of you.

Eva has also written, in case her letter has not reached you I want to tell you about her. She is a nurse ... We see each other when we can and love each other dearly.

Now about me. I am studying in a Czech school being taught by Czech lecturers. The school is in a beautiful valley, among the mountains, it's like a fairytale. I have just finished studying in form six. Tomorrow our holiday starts. I shall spend it with the Rainfords, who are as kind and as wonderful and as good to me as always. They greet you and kiss you too.

The whole school is returning to Czechoslovakia in two months' time. Otherwise, my dearest, your little Věra has grown into a chubby, happy girl who loves to learn, loves the world, but above all she loves you ... To Czechoslovakia I belong, there I want to continue my studies and to be of help. Dearest, I keep thinking of you. I know that you must have suffered dreadfully, but I believe that surrounded by our love you will forget some of

112

the suffering and will be happy again. You are the most valuable possession that we have and we long for you . . . I want to be able to tell you how much I love you, to kiss you . . .

C edric returned and my English family was complete again. The sailing boat rejoiced being back on the water.

I thanked God for Mother's and Auntie's lives, hoped that my letters would reach them, but the fear for Father pervaded my whole being.

On 13 July a letter came from Mr Herczka saying that Mother had died of typhus a week after the liberation:

Oh Mother, my darling Mother. Never shall I feel your arms around me again, kiss your hand, know you, touch you. For all your suffering I am not permitted to recompense you. Mother mine, I am sure you are in heaven and know no more pain. When will I be with you again? I shall not let you down, I shall try hard always to be the daughter you would be proud of. Just now I need so much strength, so much faith.

And Father? Where is he? Oh, God, I do not mean to grumble and complain but I do beg You for courage. And please, give it abundantly to my darling sister.

I n eight pages I conveyed to Věra, as gently as I could, our tragic news. My sister has kept one of the saddest letters I had to write. Here is a part of it:

When I look out I see the sun smiling at our world, which of late has witnessed so much suffering and sorrow. Could this be God's way of telling us that up above beauty and peace exist, that He watches over us, calling to us: 'Have faith in me and one day you will be with me. In this domain you will all be together forgetting the pain of the world.'

Are you courageous, my little sister? Have you faith and strength? I know you have, after all you are our parents' child and, in a way, mine too.

I would so like to spare you the news that I have to divulge to you, but I cannot. My darling Věra, remember that our mother has lived to see the liberation of Belsen by the English army, she rejoiced in our victory, she lived to see the end of the war. She was not in the hands of the Nazis, but in British hands, tended by kind people, when she died of typhus.

Věra, my dearest, look bravely at the heavens above and praise God for letting her live to see the end of this cruel war. You are such a good actress, do not fail in your role. To the audience that applauds you, you have to play until the curtain falls down. The acts you have to play are

113

before you, the rest of your life has to be lived. I believe that all through it, Mother will be close to you, very close to you. Can you imagine her begging God not to forsake us, to give us courage and strength, to give us faith, to let us know that one day we shall all be together again, together forever.

A nd then came a day, a day when my sick children asked, 'Why have you stopped laughing? Why are you sad? Why do you have tears in your eyes'? The day when I was given special leave. When Cedric took me gently by the hand and we sailed on the calm waters without speaking. When Roy's tears joined mine. When I had to write the hardest letter in my life to my dearest sister, repeating that our lives have to reflect all that our parents would ask of us. The day when I too cried to God, 'Why, why, oh, God, why?' The night was endless. My diary ceased on that day, when, whilst working on the children's ward, a telegram was read to me over the telephone, obliquely saying that both of my parents had died:

READ BOTH TELEGRAMS. YOUR PARENTS WERE GRAVELY ILL. THERE WAS NO HOPE. WAIT FOR FURTHER NEWS. BERTA KESTNER.

O n 27 July 1945, I wrote for the last time in my diary, the diary I had written for my parents:

Today this journal ends, for my dearest Mother and Father know it all. Now they are aware of each thought in my head, each word, every deed. Rest in peace, my dearest, may happiness surround you in the domain where suffering cannot reach you. Be joyful about us, but do not cry with us. Our lives will be dedicated to the memory of you. By the moon and the stars forever will my love soar to you – wherever you are.

PART 3

HOMECOMING

Once I knew that my parents were no more, I was unable to write more than the last short paragraph into the diaries I had kept so faithfully for them. I remember that my debate with the Almighty continued, but there was no answer to my 'why?' My dreams shattered, hopes unfulfilled, faith in question, what was I to do next? Where was my home? For a résumé of what I did do, I have to rely on some notes, some letters and on memory. I do know that among all the pain we suffered there was also strength and a determination to carry on, for the sake of those whose love would never leave their two daughters. I hoped to be able to live as they would have asked me. 'To do good is my religion,' said my father. I too had to try to live so that even in death their faith in me would not be misplaced.

I remained fiercely patriotic and was determined to return home, not only to be with Auntie Berta, who begged us to stay in England after her return to Prague, not only to be with Věra, who also chose to go home, not only to see Pepik and other friends, but because I longed to return in order to help rebuild the country that was my home. However, I acknowledged the wisdom of the advice to stay in England a few more months in order to sit my final nursing examinations, for there was no way in which I could do so in Czechoslovakia. Věra was leaving before Christmas, and so were many of her schoolmates. Having chosen to return to our homeland, we wished to get on with it. Věra's choice was to go ahead and be with our aunt, who needed our love, our youth and our faith.

The months before my departure from England are very hazy. I studied hard, I had to pass my exams and return home as a State Registered Nurse, thus I would be able to do something useful in my country. Work and study acted as a screen from the anguish and struggle in my head and heart.

In the midst of this, some time after learning of my parents' death, came a letter from our aunt. Its news I already knew, what Auntie Berta must have suffered I could hardly imagine:

My dearest, so much loved children,
I know that this letter will bring you much pain and sorrow, but
unfortunately I have to be the bearer of the most cruel news. That is, that
your dearest, by you so much loved and adored, mother, does not live
any more. She died peacefully after a horrible illness on 10 May 1945. I
was nursing her all the time, night and day I was with her. Everything I
could think of, everything I was capable of, I did for her. Unfortunately, in
the end my dearest sister Irma could fight no more and left me here – to

feel loneliness and sheer despair. It is so incredibly sad to think that after so much suffering, after the long parting from you, her children, when she has already tasted freedom brought by the English army, that your Mother should depart to eternity.

But my dear children, life seems so cruel and here all of us are sick and some will never recover. For me it is incredibly hard to write this letter, for I love you both so much. But I have decided that it is my duty to tell you about your mother's death. Both of you have grown into adulthood by now; I expect both of you have a vocation, maybe even men friends, who knows. During the six years that you have lived without us much must have occurred and much must have changed.

I do not know your plans for the future and I must not nor do I wish to influence you in any way. If you wish to return to your homeland I shall do all in my power to help you, though I am very weak at present. There is no news about your dear father, we can only hope that he is alive and that we shall see him again. However, men in concentration camps have suffered dreadfully and the majority have paid with their lives.

I am here in Bergen-Belsen Camp, and most of us will be returning to Prague in the next few days. I am not looking forward to the journey nor to the arrival in my homeland where only emptiness awaits me. Even our home is ours no more, so I do not know what I shall be doing. You will need to come back just to see if any of your property can be returned to you. I hope your friends in Čelákovice will return the possessions that your parents entrusted to their care. We can only depend on their goodwill. You must think about this, it is important to start a new life with something behind you.

I must also tell you that your father, hoping to prevent his business falling into the hands of the Germans, as all the Jewish properties had done, 'sold' your factory to Mr D, his friend, but 'sold' it on paper only. Someone informed on them and both your father and Mr D were taken away. Mr D died in a concentration camp and his wife will never give up her 'right' to your property. There are no documents to prove that I am telling the truth . . .

Eva, my dearest, forgive your old aunt for giving you news that must make you so extremely sad. Believe me that my heart is bleeding at the loss of the one being connected to me with such a pure, endlessly beautiful and, by many, much envied sisterly love. Forgive me for bringing pain to you and Věra. Be brave. Both of you are young, I am sure life holds happiness in store for you. You are fighters, you will be victorious . . .

Write to our old address in Prague, I shall get the mail no matter where I may find myself. I long to hold you both in my arms again and kiss you a thousand times.

Your so much loving auntie, Berta

I remember feeling stunned and saying, 'May God help our Auntie Berta.' She survived the unimaginable horrors of the concentration camps, how can one possibly help her to survive peace, to live on? I remembered her dry humour, her laughter, her devotion to all the members of our extended family. I knew that she could love no one more than her blind mother and her sister, our mother. How will she cope with the devastating emptiness facing her? How has she changed?

The horror of her suffering, of the suffering of our parents, of the torture of all the Jews under the Nazis, the suffering of all those whom they thought inferior, all this I absorbed slowly as news of more and more atrocities filtered into the English press. To be able to go on living, working and attempting to study for my final exam was a supreme task. I will be for ever grateful to the friends who gave their love and courage when my heart seemed empty and heavy with guilt – we had escaped so much.

I remember the night when I went to bed with my study books instead of attending a hospital dance. The night-sister saw the light in my room and entered asking, 'Why are you not at the dance, a happy thing like you?' She had not heard of the fate of my family. And this tall, strict nurse, who used to frown when she found me climbing into the nurses' home through the windows at night (I lived in awe of her), put her arms around me to express her understanding.

I remember wondering if I could ever be happy again, for the picture of my parents' agony – hungry, ill, herded in cattle tracks, existing in stables, dying – would not leave me. I thought of those who will never tell the tale, having ended their lives in gas chambers, of the children who were not allowed to live. And here I was, healthy, well fed, alive. I kept repeating to myself: 'Because of their great love for you.' For their sake I had a duty to life.

My memory is vague of the next few months. I knew I had to return, to experience living in my homeland again, to see if I was wanted, if I could help. My love and devotion to the country of my birth did not diminish with my love for the country that gave me shelter through all those turbulent years.

Parting from everyone was hard. In those days travel was difficult and leaving meant leaving for a long time. The political situation in Europe was also far from clear. Freed from Nazism, would my country escape Stalin's Communism?

I sat my exams and passed. I was now a registered nurse able to work anywhere in the world. I started packing and writing farewell letters. For some reason I have kept the copy of my note to my schoolmates from my first English school, Sandecotes, which I sent to the *School Chronicle*:

Having just finished my training in Cornelia Hospital and expecting to return to Czechoslovakia early next month, I would like to say goodbye to all my friends whom I knew at Sandecotes.

I am looking forward to seeing my country again; yet I am sorry to be leaving England. I will ever count it an honour to have had the privilege of knowing her in a time of trouble and in time of deliverance, and never cease to be thankful for the shelter England gave me, for the friends who helped me to know her and to love her. I have been very happy here and I shall not forget.

A t this time I received a letter written by Mother before she was taken to Terezín. A kind friend in our home town was guarding this letter and handed it to my sister when she thought her strong enough to accept its content. 'Be brave,' Věra wrote, 'when you read it. Yet, like me, you will shed tears when you see what a wonderful mother we had and lost.' Mother's letter was dated 1 January 1943.

My dearest children,
My life belonged to you, and you and your dearest father were the happiness of my life. I do so hope that this letter will prove not to be a farewell letter, and that the fate that tested me so cruelly will allow me to meet you and our much loved father again. I do so hope that once again we shall be able to live our lives together, full of happiness and joy.
    As a child I was already acquainted with the tragedies of this life when my mother went blind. Instead of remaining happy and carefree, I became a serious caretaker of all the household tasks. When my youngest brother was born it was me who brought him up. This was no hardship, I was young and strong, but more than that, I loved my mother and little brother with all my heart and no task on their behalf was difficult for me.
    When I was sixteen years old I met your father. Not even in my dreams did I imagine that one person can give so much love and so much happiness. My life became the happiest of fairy tales. When on 12 December 1920 we were married, I was the happiest of all human beings. Four perfect years went by and then you arrived, Eva, you who are nineteen years old today. To you I wish to say so many beautiful things, instead I have to write this sad letter, hoping that one day I shall be again permitted to press my two daughters to my aching heart and tell you everything, share everything.
    How much your father loved you, that he considered you his best friend, that he was so proud of you, Eva, you well know. You and Věra were his love and his pride. Our life with you was a life full of joy, we wished only for your happiness, and that was the reason why we summoned courage to send you into a foreign land. Four hearts felt devastated, but common sense and our faith in a better future prevailed. To start with we lived peacefully, lived for your letters. Later, only a few that arrived via the Red Cross brightened our days.
    Then 'voluntary migration' commenced. In October 1941 my brother Gustav and his family, both father's sisters and their families were taken

away by the Gestapo. This continued, and in November your beloved grandfather and Auntie Berta were taken away. Parting from them left me in agony. Yet an even greater blow afflicted me and you, my dearest children, when last year, two days after his birthday on 11 November, your father was taken away from us. I am numbed with pain; they took our kind father, who took such good care of us, whose only wish was for your happiness, who so hoped to be reunited with you again. He was our strength, our love. My dearest children, I pray so hard that the Almighty will grant us health and strength to withstand this tragedy.

For six weeks our father was kept at the country court in Boleslavy by the Gestapo, then he was transferred to the Little Fortress in Terezín. Can you imagine my life without him and without you? I thought I would go insane, leave this life; only the thought of you gives me courage to fight on, yet I do not know if I am strong enough. I wish I could wake up from this ghastly nightmare, I am confused by pain, at times I am unable to form a clear thought.

From the twelfth of last month I have been sharing a home with the two young Goldschmidt boys from next door. Their father was taken away, their mother died a year ago; we shall go together. I do not fear the departure, hopefully I might meet your father again and Auntie Berta and Grandfather and my cousin Karel and his wife; the rest of our relatives have been sent to Poland. My pain and my fear centres on father; together we wished to live, together we wished to work and, if fate so wished, together we were going to suffer. Now we have been torn apart.

I promise you, my dearest children, that I shall be brave, the thought of you and our dearest one will give me strength. But will fate grant me life to see happier days?

. . . This letter will be given to you, please hold these friends in high esteem, never forget their goodness.

And now, my dearest children, in my name and in your father's, I wish you – not only for the coming year, not only for Eva's birthday – but for the rest of your lives: be happy, be brave. We gave you so much love, we gave you the foundation for life, we so wanted to give you more, so much more. May fate make up to you all that it has taken away from us, may your lives be filled with happiness and joy. Remember your home, remember us, but do not be sad. Your whole life lies before you, life which you will share with your husbands. I bless them, I bless you and your children, even from heaven will I guard you and for your happiness will I pray. I kiss you and I bless you, Your Máma

That they had to suffer was dreadful, that they had to suffer alone was shattering, what they had to suffer was beyond my imagination. I remember being drained of tears, walking around as if dazed. What physical and mental torture they had to endure. And now there was nothing, nothing I could do to make up to them for the cruelty of fate. How much courage did it take for Mother to write such a letter. Many days went by before I divulged, or rather, felt strong enough to divulge the contents of this letter to my English family and to Roy. For my parents' sake I had to live as best I could.

Letters from home, from Auntie, from Pepik, from old schoolmates and teachers fed my eagerness to return to my homeland. The love and kindness around me filled me with sadness at the thought of leaving. I received a letter of ten pages from Mr Smith, the ex-patient who would talk to me only in Latin and with whom I still kept in touch. I was grateful for the much needed encouragement contained in his lines. Here is part of the letter:

I can vaguely imagine your grief when you realized that you would never see your parents again in this world. Remember, however, that death is not the end. It is but the entrance to a fuller life, and I know you will be buoyed up by the belief that you will be reunited with your loved ones in the Great Beyond. Meanwhile, inspired by a courage as great as that which filled the hearts of your dear parents in their last years, I know that you will strive to build your life again, to work and toil for Czechoslovakia . . . to prove to the world that the noble example set by your parents has not been in vain . . .

It was a great privilege for me to meet you and learn something of you and your country. I regard you as an Ambassadress, and freely admit that because of what I knew of you, and your high ideals, I learned to have a higher respect for Czechoslovakia than I had ever done before. I said to myself more than once, 'If this is what all Czechs are like, then it must be a great country!'

I felt very proud.

Matron's parting words were, 'We are sorry to let you go, but remember, if you don't find things to your liking at home you can always come back. I think you are very brave.' Mrs Allner said as she kissed me goodbye, 'You might have made a happy home with others, but I don't think you could find anyone who would love you more.' And Mrs Allner senior added, 'You have been the bright spot of this horrible war, a real treasure.'

So many more wrote and spoke kind words to me. Roy came with me from Poole to London and our parting was sad. Roy whispered, 'I shall always be happy when thinking of you. You will be welcome back whenever it may be.'

I spent a night with Rita Somogyi, who took me to the train that carried me to Folkestone. Here I boarded the boat for Calais and waved farewell to the White Cliffs of Dover as they disappeared in the distance. From Calais I went by train to Brussels, then Aachen, Nuremberg and on to Czechoslovakia. In Prague, on the platform, stood my sister with the tragic figure of Auntie Berta. The tears of joy at our reunion mingled with the tears of grief for those who were not allowed to live to witness this moment.

Věra was the first to hear what actually happened to our parents. Not until I returned home, not until I wrestled with the incredible void in my heart left by our parents' absence, not until then did my sister reveal to me what she had learnt.

On 13 November 1942, our father was taken to the Little Fortress of Terezín, where he was tortured. A little later Mother, still at home, received a note smuggled out of Terezín asking her to give a large sum of money to a certain Nazi officer. Hoping that she was helping Father, Mother did as instructed. In January 1943 Mother was herded into a cattle truck with the rest of the Jewish families in our district to be taken to Terezín, the Jewish ghetto. They were crammed in and were hardly able to breathe, but when my distressed and bewildered mother saw the light of day again, there, in the crowd of prisoners, stood Father. White-haired and much older looking – the tortures he suffered imprinted on his face – he was without his nails, but alive. As a result of the bribe, Father had been transferred from the dreadful Fortress to the less punishing Ghetto. To live together was forbidden, but our parents could meet. Mother shared her meagre food rations with Father. He was a heavy smoker and whenever he could he swapped his food for a cigarette. Father remained weak and ill. Mercifully our grandmother died at home before Grandfather and Auntie Berta were taken to Terezín. Like many other old people in the cold comfortless barracks, Grandfather almost lost his reason. To be with him, Mother and Auntie volunteered for the gruelling work in dreadful conditions of looking after the mentally ill. Fortunately, death claimed our grandfather a few weeks later.

Then Auntie was sent to Auschwitz. She was followed by Father and in January 1944 Mother joined them. However, in Camp B-11b contact between male and female prisoners was forbidden. One large dilapidated stable housed 500 prisoners. Many died from starvation and the bitter cold. Sickness afflicted everyone, and none escaped hard labour except the thousands who were marched straight into gas chambers. June 1944 witnessed the liquidation of Camp B-11b by the murderer 'Dr' Mengele. Our parents and Auntie were not among the 7000 men and women and children whose lives ended in the gas chambers. After parading naked in front of Mengele, Mother and Auntie were transported to a concentration camp in Hamburg, Father to Bleck-hammer Camp in Silesia. Only a few survived the appalling conditions in Silesia. Father was not one of them. That was all we learnt of his fate.

In Hamburg Mother was 'privileged'. A fantastic cook, she was chosen to display her culinary art in the officers' mess. Soon she was displaced by a younger Jewess and joined Auntie in the heavy work of labourers. But the short time in the kitchen supplied her with extra food, which she diligently shared with her sister as well as other prisoners.

Before the end of March 1945 the few survivors were taken to Bergen-Belsen, and were left there without food or medication. On 15 April, the British army entered the camp and many said that the sight confronting them was harder to bear than anything else during this cruel war. Thousands of prisoners died before liberation, many died later. Among the latter were our two cousins from Prague and our mother. All three died in Auntie Berta's arms.

The only thing that brought our parents comfort was the thought of us and the certainty that by sending us away they had saved our lives. Auntie kept saying this over and over again, knowing the guilt we carried for having escaped the torture and perhaps death. She also asked why should she have been spared when her loved ones died. So frail, so lonely, how could we ever help her to carry her burden?

In England I hoped, now I almost despaired. Those for whom I prayed and longed for six years were not there – a witness to their suffering as well as her own was my aunt. I attempted to push out of my mind the realization of all they had to endure, in order that I could live and go on living without hate. Perhaps that is the reason why the time spent in my country after the war is only dimly imprinted on my memory. I went to Čelákovice, the home town I had dreamt of. I met old friends, whose talk about our parents who were much loved left me in tears as well as warming my heart. I remember thinking that Mother and Father would never really die as their memory was so alive, not only in our hearts but also in the remembrance of those who were touched by my parents' generosity.

I met Pepik again on Mstětická Silnice, the place where we had parted. Our reunion was happy; our fondness for each other had survived the parting. Yet there was much to learn about each other; we parted as children and met as adults. Only the future would show how our relationship would evolve. Pepik was now in the army, and we could meet only when he was given leave. During the war, Pepik finished his studies in a business college and later worked in a factory; being a Roman Catholic, he escaped the fate of the Jews.

Some of our friends gladly returned the possessions that Mother had entrusted to their safekeeping before the Gestapo forced her to leave her home; others denied ever having been given anything. We could do little, even if we saw the large picture from our living-room hanging on their wall, or met a member of their family wearing Mother's winter coat when Auntie Berta had none. I did not cry for the loss of property, but I did cry with joy when I was given back my bicycle. It looked as perfect as it did on my last Christmas at home. The guardians of my bike were poor in material things, but how rich in kindness!

In Čelákovice bitter-sweet memories took hold of me, especially when I managed to escape on my own into the fields; the tears were never far from my eyes. I kept repeating to myself that when we cry we cry for ourselves, for our dear ones are resting in peace and for them we have to live and laugh.

One act I could not face: to enter our old home, now occupied by strangers. I would sit under the flowering oak trees surrounding an uneven cobbled road that ran through the village square. I would gaze at the town hall and drink water from the village pump. Every time our grandfather paid us a visit he demanded this nectar. And when I turned my back to the hall, my gaze fell on a row of little houses. One was a small farm: from here I used to carry in a large jug fresh, creamy milk. The next building housed my piano teacher. Sadly, I remembered the day when I stood on this village square after my piano lesson, my whole being overflowing with the joy of living. My gaze would reach the end of the village meadow and where our house stood. Opposite the house was the little pub where Father used to play chess until the early hours of the morning. My gaze also embraced the two houses of the other Jewish families, four adults and three children altogether, all of them perished in concentration camps.

But not all was sadness. In Čelákovice I, never a good dancer, found myself swept away on my feet to the tune of Czech music by the boys I used to share a school bench with. Pepik would come whenever his army duties permitted, and he was eager to build our future together on the dreams of youthful love. I was not ready, and thought that I did not really know the man he had become, and that the girl in his arms was also a stranger to him. I remembered the merry-go-round that used to be part of the monthly fair in our little town, and I felt as if I was sitting on the little seat being whirled around, unable to take charge of my destiny.

In Čelákovice both Věra and I found a kind of peace. After the intensity of our relationship in England, I do not remember us sharing much in Prague, Věra had her friends and I had mine.

So used to writing a diary, I again wrote little notes, some of which are still in my possession:

At times I find Prague oppressive, but Čelákovice remains my home. There by the river Elbe where fields and meadows overflow to the far horizon, I feast my eyes on the gentle rocking corn – the colour of gold – dotted by blue cornflowers and red poppies. How often have I dreamt of this picture in England!

In Čelákovice, Věra and I are welcomed and loved, perhaps more for our parents' sake than our own. I do thank God for kind people and for the privilege given me to meet so many of them. My dearest parents, you had hearts of gold. I do wish I could inherit a tiny bit of your kindness and magnanimity.

Auntie refused to come with us to Čelákovice. She loved Prague; the little solace she could find she found in her home town. She also enjoyed meeting Honza Pacovský, who was now working in a Prague hospital. We talked of England and compared notes. Honza was going to be married, but still felt himself a stranger among his own people. How well I understood. He advised me to look for a position in industry, where as a nurse tending the sick and injured I would be contributing to the economic recovery of my nation. I accepted his advice.

I found a job as an industrial nurse in a factory in Prague. I remember enjoying my work and the company of my workmates. The hardest part was learning the names of the medication – I knew what they were in English but not in Czech. Hard concentration was required so as not to poison my patients!

The blight on my horizon was the increasing proclamation of allegiance to Communism and the belittling of England. I remember being on the main street of Prague, Václavské Náměstí, when thousands of people were marching declaring the glory of Russia as their saviour. I felt then how easy it was to be swayed by crowds. I also felt that England's role was neglected in the thanksgiving. When one day our neighbour shouted at Auntie: 'It is a pity that all the Jews did not perish in the concentration camps,' I thought my heart would break, for Auntie's sake rather than Věra's and mine. Was this the home I dreamt of, longed for? I felt I belonged, and yet I did not belong.

Home to us was a small flat, less than half of the residence that my grandparents used to occupy. Even the bathroom was not allotted to Auntie, only a dark bedroom and Grandmother's kitchen. Věra and Auntie slept in the bedroom, I on a mattress in the kitchen. It was not the smallness of the place but the hostility from the occupant of the other part of the residence that made living hard for the three of us. The housing situation in Prague was difficult for those returning home as their homes by now were occupied by others. When Auntie came back from Belsen, she was compelled to live with her cousin Karel and his wife Míla, who also returned from a concentration camp. Their small flat was bulging at the seams when my sister joined them. As Míla was expecting a baby a few months later, it seemed imperative that Auntie and Věra found other accommodation. Auntie was legally entitled to her old flat, from which she was forcibly removed by the Nazis. However, as that accommodation belonged also to her parents and she was the only one of the original occupants left alive, her entitlement was only one single room, and the smallest one at that. Věra told me how hard she had to fight at the housing office for this little gesture. As Auntie by then was Věra's legal guardian and Věra was living with her, the authorities grudgingly allocated her the tiny kitchen. They refused to take into account the fact that I would be joining them in a few weeks. Apparently the butcher who had taken the flat kept Grandfather's best furniture and left Auntie his cast-offs.

This was not the fair play Věra and I were accustomed to in England. I kept thinking of Father's letter in which he bid us to stay in England should our country reject us. I did not experience rejection directly and except for that one instance with the butcher I did not experience anti-Semitism against me as a person, but somehow it hung in the air. Those who occupied homes and held on to Jewish properties were loath to give them up to those who returned. Věra complained of being discriminated against at school in subtle ways, such as being awarded lower marks than she knew she had a right to. Now and then the most unexpected person would refer to someone in a derogatory way, saying, 'he is a Jew' not realizing I was one too. And more than that, I was one who had returned from the safety of England, returned because I thought myself to be a Czech.

Auntie looked tired and sad, but never complained. She loved to sit on a bench in a park, warmed by the sun and watching children at play. For better or for worse, Prague was her city. The buildings were more shabby than when she was taken away, but on the whole Prague was almost untouched by bombs. The hundreds of towers of which her city boasted seemed like hundreds of arms reaching to the sky. From its position on the hillside, the magnificent castle of Hradčany gazed at the beauty underneath. Vltava; to the English known as the river Moldau, spiralled through the township to disappear in the distance. Spanned by a number of bridges, the most outstanding of them Karl's Bridge, the river was graced with majestic statues on each side. Prague was as I remembered it, and so was Čelákovice. That is, except for our house, which in reality was far more shabby than in my dreams. Knowing of our affection for our home town, Auntie never objected to being left alone on most weekends. In retrospect, perhaps she appreciated having her home to herself.

Věra and I brought our young friends home. Auntie Berta loved young people, and now and then the old sparkle would appear in her eyes, which most of the time projected the sorrow of her soul. Auntie appreciated being a surrogate parent to Věra. I lost my role and my sister and I stood equal. Cheering up Auntie was for both of us a difficult task.

Four months after my arrival in Czechoslovakia I was asked to accompany 200 Czech children to England. These children were to recuperate in English homes, but prior to entering the homes one month had to be spent in quarantine. During that time the children needed a nurse who could speak Czech as well as English. A friend working in the Government approached me, stressing that I was their ideal choice. As she also received permission for me to take leave of absence from my work-place, I finally accepted this offer after some deliberation.

I remember to this day being surprised on parting from the director of the company I worked for when he said to me, 'Do not feel guilty on our behalf should you choose not to come back. I wish you much happiness in all that you do.' I mused, 'How strange. I am coming back, I am going for only one month.'

Though Auntie encouraged me to go to England, she was sad and parted as if she was never to see me again. 'But I am going for only four weeks, with a small suitcase, leaving all my possessions behind,' I stressed. I could not understand.

However, I understood after a short time in England, for here the situation facing my country was clear. By friends old and new I was told, 'You have escaped one dictator, Hitler. Do you wish to live under another one, Stalin? Do you think that is what your parents would wish for you?' The clouds gathering on the horizon indicated only too clearly that once again a dictator would rule over my land.

Auntie and Věra urged me to stay. Pepik threatened that if I didn't return he would marry the first girl he met. He did.

Still bruised by my parents' death, dazed by all that had happened since, loving friends in two lands and devoted to both countries, I chose England as my refuge for a second time. My predominant reasons for doing so were that if Czechoslovakia did not fall under Stalin's domination I would be able to return and to work for my country. If it did then I must be in a position to help Auntie and Věra to get out. Two years later I did help my sister to return to England when the situation at home became too dangerous for her. Auntie, though demanding that Věra go, refused to leave. In Prague there were a few friends who had suffered as she had done, there she had her small pension, and memories that brought her loved ones closer. There she belonged.

I realized how much 'at home' I felt in England when once again the Allners welcomed me with open arms – as did Roy and other friends. I turned back to nursing, first in my hospital in Poole, later in London. I disliked large cities, but Věra wrote from Czechoslovakia that she would train as a nurse in order to obtain a permit to re-enter England. This compelled me to search for a hospital where I could further my education whilst Věra participated in the nursing school of the same hospital. Thus I enrolled us both in a London hospital and sadly left my friends and old haunts. However, on her arrival in England, Věra informed me that she would never do such work, and with the help of her friends started a typing course. I was hurt, but understood her point. Nevertheless, I stayed in London and a year later emerged a fully fledged midwife.

Less than a year after her return, Věra married an Englishman and lived in London. So I saw a great deal of my sister and was able to be with her when her first child was born.

Old friends and new brightened my days, and were kind enough to say that I brightened theirs. So used to holding on to my feelings when I was with him, I was unable to reciprocate Roy's affection in the way he longed for. As always, he understood. Had I failed? Where did I belong? For six years I had lived for my parents, I hardly knew how to live for myself. The confusion in my head was matched only by the confusion in my heart.

That was until, in Mile End Hospital, over an armful of bed pans, I met the man I eventually married. Michael was a medical student, I a trainee midwife. We were married in Mr and Mrs Allner's little church. I walked to the altar on the arm of my 'Big Man', with Bunty's son Peter as my charming page boy. To crown the day, among the guests were Mr Jones the gardener and Mr Wiltshire the waiter from Sandecotes. I cried with joy and fervently wished that somehow somewhere the parents I so much loved would witness my happiness.

My happiness was complete when our two children filled our lives. They have compensated many times over for any sorrow I suffered in the past. I was so blessed, I had so much to live for. I never took this for granted – for others had suffered and died, whilst I survived.

After seven years in England we emigrated to New Zealand. Like many Englishmen Michael was tempted to explore other lands. Our deliberation was decided by the Suez Crisis and its threat to peace. We chose to move our children out of Europe to what we hoped to be a safer part of the globe. My departure was more than tinged with sadness when parting from Věra and all my friends. The world was getting smaller in 1957 and travel easier, except to my country behind the Iron Curtain. It was not until a few years later that Auntie was able to travel freely to England.

In New Zealand we were met by kind and friendly people. This beautiful country was to be our new home. When Michael eventually settled in general practice, I was able to help. An old dream I had was also fulfilled when I became a student at the university, after both my children had finished their studies there. I emerged with a Bachelor of Arts degree and three years later with a Master of Arts (Hons). As my son remarked, I am a late developer.

I felt no need to visit the country of my birth. On my travels to England I would meet Auntie Berta at Věra's, where she was a regular visitor. Being 'British' and living in New Zealand, I wanted to forget the pain of the six turbulent wartime years, forget that I was born Jewish, forget that I was Czech – those memories were associated with sorrow, with loss, with despair. My children were to grow up in their father's faith and belong wholly to his world unburdened by their mother's past. The past that was buried and forgotten. Or so I thought.

One cannot escape one's past, it will not be abandoned. I never said goodbye to my homeland in 1946, thinking I would return. I never said goodbye to my parents in 1939, believing in our reunion. Their bodies were not buried in known graves adorned by flowers of remembrance. Their grave was in my heart.

Years later, I felt a need to see my country again, and in 1978 the time came. Overcome by a feverish need to return, I flew to Czechoslovakia. I was met by Auntie Berta, living in a tiny flat in Prague. The flat we had shared with her was considered to be too large by the authorities after Věra and I left.

My mother's sister was still anxious, but so brave and so kind. She would distribute nearly all the gifts given her among her friends. I had written diligently to her from New Zealand, but she refused to face the journey to the other side of the world. Věra and her visits were her anchor, and later my children never missed calling on her when in Europe.

On my return journey to Czechoslovakia, a sorrow gripped me with a force that I was unable to understand and unable to shake off. For me that month in Czechoslovakia was a most excruciating experience. I would never have believed that one can relive the past again, but I did; I saw my parents everywhere, their ghosts would not leave me.

At a school reunion, there were these rotund middle-aged people, but my vision presented me with a picture of young schoolchildren of the year 1939. I met Pepik with his charming wife, walked in the lanes among the fields and visited Mstětická Silnice. I was young again, I felt the past, I suffered the past – it embraced me, held me. Even now I was unable to walk through the doors of what used to be our house. My friend Máňa could not understand why I ran away and why I shed bitter tears. I could not explain my feelings to anyone, least of all to myself.

129

Proud of her city, Auntie re-introduced me to the streets of our beautiful Prague, and I tried to hide from her the torment I felt. She was such a lonely figure at the airport when I left her. I said goodbye to her, to my country and, in a way, to my parents. As I flew to England the heaviness left me as if by magic.

I knew then that I had had to relive the past again, that I had had to spend that month so mingled with pain in order to accept the past as part of my experience, remember it – nay, treasure it – yet refuse to allow it to interfere with the present. At that moment I also realized that I could deny neither my Jewishness, for which my parents suffered, nor my Czech heritage, for I belonged to that little nation where my childhood knew so much happiness. I was flying to England, and England had saved my life. There I had spent the years when I grew into womanhood, there I laughed and loved and shed bitter tears. I had been a victim, but a fortunate victim. So part of my heart had to remain not only in the country of my birth but also in the country of my deliverance.

A few days later, I flew to the country of my choice, which is my home and has been for the last thirty-three years, to the country so far removed from the troubles of Europe, which like a long white cloud nestles in blue seas. I am content among the people of this land, free in the hills and mountains surrounded by the oceans. With the rest of New Zealanders I praise and chastise and argue about issues affecting us. To me that is a mark of belonging. I am 'a Kiwi with an accent', I shall never lose my Czech lilt.

Both my children have grown up here, my little grandson was born here. Remembering the past, I feel the pain affecting so many children of this world because of mankind's folly, cruelty, and ignorance. I only hope that they will also experience the other side of human nature from which love goes forth to give strength and courage to all.

FIFTY YEARS ON

My son Simon lives in Denmark and gravitates to Prague whenever possible. His travel books on Czechoslovakia confirm his allegiance to his mother's country. When there, Simon never fails to visit Pepik and his wife, with whom I keep in touch. I am fortunate that at present my daughter and her husband are living in Auckland. Their son Jeff is the reason for my being the world's proudest grandmother. My children and their partners were the last to see Auntie Berta before her death in 1981. Her letters testify to her lasting delight at meeting them.

Věra lives in London. Her three children and three grandchildren as well as many friends fill her life.

Roy's marriage took place nearly two years after mine, and he haunts the places we used to visit in a car instead of on a bicycle.

Mr and Mrs Allner departed from this world many years ago, and Bunty lives alone in the house that opened its doors to me as her family opened their hearts. I corresponded with Miss Dunn and Miss Vinall until their deaths. Mr Herczka remained in England, a permanent refugee. He was cared for by a friend of his and died a few years after the war ended.

I did not set out to write a book, only to translate my diaries and perhaps explain their mother to my children, and thus enable them to touch that part of their inheritance. Instead of fitting a narrative into chapters, I had to adapt chapters into the sequence of my diaries.

I agreed to the publication of this material to show the agony as well as the strength of a teenager in the midst of comparative plenty. A teenager whose God was unable to explain to her the cruelty of man to man. The translation has been an arduous journey into the past. When reading what my own hand had written, I have not only been transported on the wings of memory to scenes of fifty years ago, I have also relived the most powerful six years of my life, which so affected the rest of my life. I have felt the pain again. At times I was very angry with the youngster called Eva, though I sympathized with her lonely struggle to grasp the world and the meaning of life and love.

Being a parent myself, I understand what my father meant when he wrote: 'To love one's child is the culmination of one's life.' That is my gift to my children, which they will pass on to their children. This great gift, received so abundantly from my parents, will for ever remain part of my being, gracing the joys and struggles of my life. Thus my mother and father live on in my memory, for, like a beacon, in a secret corner of my heart, my love shines for them.